The Development of European Civilization

Kenneth R. Bartlett, Ph.D.

D0920728

THE
GREAT
COURSES®

PUBLISHED BY:

THE GREAT COURSES
Corporate Headquarters
4840 Westfields Boulevard, Suite 500
Chantilly, Virginia 20151-2299
Phone: 1-800-832-2412
Fax: 703-378-3819
www.thegreatcourses.com

Kenneth R. Bartlett, Ph.D.
Professor of History and Renaissance Studies
University of Toronto

Professor Kenneth R. Bartlett is a Professor of History and Renaissance Studies at the University of Toronto. He received his Ph.D. from the University of Toronto in 1978. He was the first director of the University of Toronto Art Centre and founding director of the Office of Teaching Advancement at the university, a position he held until 2009.

Much of Professor Bartlett's career has been devoted to bringing the culture of European history into the undergraduate and graduate classroom. He has taught regularly in the University of Toronto Summer Abroad Programs in Europe. He has been the recipient of numerous teaching awards, most notably the 3M Teaching Fellowship, awarded by the Canadian Society for Teaching and Learning in Higher Education, and the inaugural President's Teaching Award from the University of Toronto. In 2007, Professor Bartlett was one of the 10 finalists in TVOntario's Best Lecturer competition, which pits students' favorite instructors against one another in a battle of charisma, clarity, passion, and conviction; that same year, he was recognized with an inaugural Leadership in Faculty Teaching Award by the government of Ontario.

In addition to having produced two highly acclaimed series for The Great Courses, Professor Bartlett is the author of *The English in Italy, 1525–1558: A Study in Culture and Politics* (1991); *The Civilization of the Italian Renaissance* (1992); and *Humanism and the Northern Renaissance* (with M. McGlynn, 2000). He is also coeditor or translator of 4 other books and author of more than 35 articles and chapters on European history and culture. In 2003, he was cocurator of the exhibition *Gods, Saints and Heroes: Italian Renaissance Maiolica from the Metropolitan Museum of Art* at the Gardiner Museum. In addition, Professor Bartlett has been the academic consultant on the Illuminated Filmworks videos about the Vatican Library, for the television series *The Naked Archaeologist*, as well as for international exhibitions at the Art Gallery of Ontario.

Professor Bartlett lives in Toronto, Ontario, with his wife, Gillian. ∎

Table of Contents

Table of Contents

Table of Contents

Table of Contents

Table of Contents

The Development of European Civilization

Scope:

E urope is a continent of ideas as well as events. This course traces the development of European civilization from the Middle Ages until 1939 by investigating the interdependency between ideas and action, ideology and practice, theory and events. A great many of the still-dynamic perspectives on the world arose in Europe, making that continent a laboratory for the conditions and ideas that animate the modern world.

Concepts such as fundamental human rights, democracy, capitalism, liberalism, nationalism, socialism, communism, and fascism were created in Europe, for better or worse, and those ideas defined the character of the modern age. The voyages of discovery, the Reformation, the Scientific Revolution, the Enlightenment, and the Industrial Revolution emerged in response to complex political, social, and economic conditions unique to Europe. We trace these events, investigate their causes and effects, and evaluate how Europe became not only a laboratory for ideas but a bloody theater of war and political experimentation. We also follow the biographies of men and women who defined these events and trace the rise and fall of institutions and nations.

Pervasive principles, such as European unity, can be seen in structures as diverse as the Holy Roman Empire, the universal Catholic Church, and the European Union; and continuing tensions between individual and collective responsibility and the nature of the state itself are revealed in the theoretical and political divisions on the continent over its long history. What emerge sfrom these 48 lectures is a narrative of the mind and experience of Europe, a continent that became the engine of the modern world and the repository of Western culture. ∎

The Idea and Place of Europe

Lecture 1

Europe is not only a place but an idea and a memory. The political, social, economic, cultural, and intellectual experience of Europeans has influenced every part of the world, spread through contact, conversion, and emigration of peoples from the continent to the four corners of the planet.

Until very recently, Europe has been a major exporter of surplus population and the languages and culture of the emigrants have defined the experience in North and South America, Australia and New Zealand, and significantly influenced every other nation on Earth.

For those of us living in North America, our institutions, culture, and collective unconscious derive from that continent and its history. Moreover, as a consequence of past exploration, conversion, and colonization, many of these same ideas and structures have established roots elsewhere and continue today to enjoy either a close kinship or a dynamic tension with the states and peoples of Europe.

Within Europe itself there have been fundamental shifts of principle and a variety of experience that make any general statements about the continent misleading. Constitutionally, for example, there have always been republics as well as monarchies. Ideologically, there have been totalitarian dictatorships and liberal democracies. Both socialism and capitalism were born from and transformed by events in Europe. The Scientific Revolution and the Enlightenment are largely European constructs. So, too, are rationalism and industrialism.

From the Crusades to the voyages of discovery to the mass emigration of millions to the New World, Europe has exported and expanded its influence. Its various "isms" have galvanized thinkers, politicians, and activists in every corner of the globe. In short, Europe created the platform on which our modern experience was constructed.

Europe has been called the violent continent for good reason: As many of our lectures will reveal, war was often used as an instrument of policy. But the two world wars were so unspeakable in their carnage and destruction that Europeans have recently moved away from war to ensure that such events will no longer occur.

It is important, therefore, to look at the development of European civilization as a vehicle for determining not only who we are, but also where we might be going and what we might become. We need to see how and why certain ideas were developed and applied. Finally, we need to look at Europe both as the experience of a large number of independent states, each with its own traditions, and as a collectivity, that is, as an idea—the idea of Europe.

The modern European Union has its roots in the posturing of Napoleon's adventurism, the expansionist ambitions of the Holy Roman Empire, the Catholic (meaning "universal") Church and the memory of the ancient Roman Empire. The concept of Europe remains alive, and its story is the narrative both of conflict and of cooperation. Understanding this history in so many ways leads to a better understanding of ourselves. ■

When we talk about institutions like parliamentary or representative democracy, we're talking about a set of principles that developed on the European continent.

den Boer, *The History of the Idea of Europe.*

Pagden, *The Idea of Europe.*

Questions to Consider

1. In this age of global perspective, is it still useful to have a course centered solely on Europe?

2. Before our course begins, describe your current perceptions of Europe.

Feudalism and the Medieval World
Lecture 2

The collapse of Roman Imperial rule in the West in the 5ᵗʰ century resulted in a period of general chaos made worse by waves of invading barbarian tribes and the disintegration of trade and communication routes in Europe. Famine and plague joined warfare to ravage the western provinces and homeland of Rome. As a result, there was a pressing need for alternate forms of security and government.

Individuals and groups sought the protection of powerful men, often owners of vast estates, who could fulfill the responsibilities of administration and justice, as well as offer protection. The origins of this new order lay deep in the Roman relationship between patrons and clients—a relationship that dated from Republican times. Clients had traditionally met powerful Romans, such as senators, at their homes and accompanied them throughout the city. In return, these patrons provided their clients with jobs, assistance, some status of their own, and protection if necessary.

The barbarian tribes brought with them their own forms of social, political, and military organization, based on personal bonds that attached favored retainers to prominent warriors. But the traditions of Rome remained available for adoption by those Romanized barbarians who had embraced Christianity and revered the potency of the now lost empire.

These traditions merged when the ancient Mediterranean patron/client relationship of the Romans met the tribal practice of the warrior chieftains who enjoyed the service and support of an elite band of retainers, or **comitatus**. Richly privileged, loyal through self-interest and sworn fidelity, powerful and experienced in war, this chosen elite functioned as leaders in battle and administrators in peace.

When the stirrup was introduced into Europe from the East, it became possible—thanks to increased stability—for heavily armed warriors to fight on horseback. But the armor, training, and horses this required were expensive, and their use fell to the elite warriors who served the tribal kings. The economic collapse of Rome in the West meant there was insufficient coinage to pay for such service. On the other hand, land was plentiful and cheap. Consequently, kings and chieftains began the practice of granting estates to sustain an elite class of knights. These estates meant power, status, and wealth sufficient to support mounted warriors.

As the chaos in Europe continued and spread during the 7th–11th centuries, more and more professional knights were needed.

As the chaos in Europe continued and spread during the 7th–11th centuries, more and more professional knights were needed and more land was transferred to sustain them. The result was a continent hugely fragmented among a great many members of the knightly elite—a fragmentation that reduced the overall authority of the king or chief. This was feudalism: public power in private hands, little enforceable central authority, and the creation of an elite class of landholding warriors who were increasingly seen as a hereditary caste, or nobility. ■

Important Term

comitatus: Band of privileged retainers in service to a barbarian chieftain.

Suggested Reading

Bartlett, *The Making of Europe: Conquest, Colonization and Cultural Change, 950–1350.*

Moore, *The First European Revolution, 970–1215.*

Lecture 2: Feudalism and the Medieval World

1. Was the flight to armed security the only possible response of Europeans after the collapse of the Roman Empire?

2. Why were urban Europeans more exposed to danger than rural Europeans when the Roman imperial system fell?

The Three Orders of Medieval Society
Lecture 3

Although no complex society can be structured into neat categories, the society of Medieval Europe can be seen as conforming to a tripartite model containing three conditions: the first estate of the clergy, the second estate of the nobility, and the third estate of all those who worked in a manual capacity.

The clergy were charged with ministering to the faithful to ensure their salvation and spiritual comfort. The lowest ranks of the secular clergy occasionally had to work the lands attached to their churches to augment their meager tithes, and many orders of regular clergy included labor in their monastic rules. Nevertheless, this was a privileged class exempt from normal taxation and operating under the **canon law** of the Church rather than temporal jurisdictions.

The second estate of the nobility provided protection, government, and justice for those over whom they ruled. This, too, was a privileged class with sufficient land to sustain the heavy burdens of constant training and preparation for war. The possession of high status, the ability to practice patronage, and the exercise of power meant the nobility was seen as the pre-eminent class in medieval secular society. Its values and practices were idealized in the concept of a chivalric world and celebrated in art and literature.

Finally, there were the people who worked with their hands, rather than enjoying the fruits of others' labor. This third estate constituted over 90 percent of the population of Europe in the Middle Ages. It, too, was hierarchical and variegated inasmuch as it contained serfs bound to the soil of manors, urban laborers and artisans, skilled craftsmen, and wealthy professionals, as well as the occasional wealthy international merchant.

However, great riches could not erase the lack of status or privilege. The poorest knight enjoyed more social recognition than the richest merchant, and the very fact of having made one's own way and one's own fortune cemented the inferiority attached to labor. All taxation fell on the third estate, both in terms of cash payments and labor services; and justice was by no means blind to class and influence.

Leisure was a mark of privilege and status. The nobility and clergy did work in the broad sense of the term, but their work was defined in such a way as to reflect the hierarchical values of the time. The feudal and manorial systems provided the economic base for the two upper classes to live in leisure by guaranteeing the nobility and clergy the ownership of land and control over the lives and labor of those who worked it.

During the High Middle Ages, economic changes improved the material, even the legal, position of the rural poor.

During the High Middle Ages, economic changes improved the material, even the legal, position of the rural poor. Peasants gained some degree of mobility, and improvements to agriculture eased some of the problems of famine, though the depredations of war or sickness remained.

By the Later Middle Ages, the urban classes had grown in number and influence. The urban population became an important stimulus for change, as it did not fit neatly into the tripartite division of society. ∎

Important Term

canon law: The law of and governing the Roman Catholic Church.

Suggested Reading

Kaeuper, *Chivalry and Violence in Medieval Europe*.

Tuchman, *A Distant Mirror*.

1. Was the imperative for social mobility the most important factor in the decline of the tripartite social structure of medieval Europe?

2. Chivalry became the dominant culture of the High Middle Ages: do all dominant social and economic groups impose their values on their society?

The Manorial Economy
Lecture 4

Insufficient coinage and localized allegiance meant that the organization of agriculture became the economic foundation of most of the continent. In fact, agriculture employed the vast majority of Europeans in the Middle Ages, with no one altogether outside its economy.

In the early Middle Ages, from 400 to 700, the population of Europe dramatically declined, and European agriculture stagnated. The period of the 9th–11th centuries, however, saw significant innovations in agriculture—such as three-crop rotation and the invention of the horse collar—and the beginnings of a population increase. Between 85–95 percent of the population of medieval Western Europe was engaged in farming as their principle activity.

Medieval agriculture was cooperative. Europe was organized into manors, self-sufficient estates able to support one heavily-armed mounted knight and his retainers. Every manor was much the same, consisting of a village of peasants, more or less tied to the land they tilled, and communal structures, such as a church, an oven, a mill, and a smithy. The baker, miller, blacksmith, and priest were not paid for their services in cash but received payment in kind. Indeed, the genius of the manorial system was that it developed as an economic organization that functioned without money.

The peasants tilled the land in narrow strips to ensure that no one family got the most arable soil. In addition they all farmed the landlord's fields, or the demesne—manorial land that a feudal lord kept for his own private use. The entire harvest of this large plot was given to the landlord, together with a share of the peasants' own harvest. The landlord occupied a fortified house on the manor, suitable for offering protection and from which he administered justice.

Although almost every manor in Europe adhered to this basic organization, each had its own customary practices. These determined the level of freedom enjoyed by the peasants, the payment due the landlord, and fees for special functions such as marriage. In a world without enforceable laws and only local authority, this customary tradition provided the only protection the poor could rely on when challenged by the strong.

Thus, by the 11th century, Western Europe was politically fragmented into small units, ruled by a professional warrior class, who obeyed no laws but their own principles of feudal practice and custom, known as chivalry. Although the Church knew that it could not turn these professional killing machines into men of peace, it also knew that their power and aggression could be turned against the enemies of Christendom. It is not an accident, then, that the Crusades erupted at just the time when these principles of chivalry were beginning.

Innovations like horse collars allowed farmers to use horses as opposed to oxen in farming, furthering the population growth.

With chivalry and the ideal of courtly love, the feudal nobility began to develop into an aristocracy, with more of an emphasis on culture and a luxurious way of life. Mutual obligations, personal loyalty, customary regulations, and cooperative agriculture all began to be undermined by the introduction of an element for which the system was not designed: money. ∎

Suggested Reading

Duby, *Rural Economy and Country Life in the Medieval West.*

Lopez, *The Commercial Revolution of the Middle Ages, 950–1350.*

Questions to Consider

1. What effect did the introduction of a money economy have on the structure of feudal society?

2. Are there examples of public power in private hands today?

The Growth of Trade and Towns
Lecture 5

> The rise of urban life, long distance trade, and a money economy
> were the factors that first challenged and then corroded the rural,
> subsistence, localized feudal world. The development of trade and a
> money economy permitted people living in towns to develop wealth
> and power to the point that they could ultimately join in the undoing
> of feudal fragmentation by assisting a central authority—like the
> king—in establishing power and weakening the resistance of the
> fractious nobility.

The increasing demand for luxury goods among the feudal nobility damaged their economic power and introduced a cash economy that undermined the manorial system. Inflation affected everyone. Grain prices rose faster than wages throughout the late medieval period. Mutual obligations, personal loyalty, customary regulations, cooperative agriculture all began to be undermined by the introduction of money into the system.

The revival of Roman legal practices, particularly those that aided the central authority, also served to undermine the foundations on which feudalism rested. Enforceable contracts and legal regulation were essential to the rise of towns and trade. The establishment of uniform systems of justice provided an alternative to the use of knightly force for settling disputes. Royal courts became the highest courts, and local manor courts could be overruled by them.

Improvements in communication, education, and the overall economic situation led to a growth of towns. This, coupled with the centralizing example of the Roman Catholic Church, began to direct Western Europe away from feudalism and toward great centralized authority.

Europe became a more dynamic continent. Population increased, bolstering the demand for more trade and coinage. When Pope Urban II preached the First Crusade in 1095, he used the vocabulary of religious zeal, but these adventures were also a response to the growing ambitions and pressures of

European societies. Thus the Crusades were both cause and effect of the explosion of trade in the 12th century and the expansion of Europe.

The luxury trade through Italy reconnected the long distance trade routes of the Mediterranean and re-created a culture and structure of trade, including reliable coinage and commercial law. Changes in business practices altered the economic relations between Europeans and reshaped the political and social structure of the continent. A natural use of money was banking, and the great Florentine banking families made huge fortunes in the 13th and 14th centuries.

One advantage of the Roman Empire was that everybody recognized the value of Roman coins.

The impact of the Black Death in 1348 was staggering. It encouraged the movement of artisans, laborers, and agricultural workers in search of lower rents and higher wages. It also concentrated wealth in the hands of fewer people. Kings found solid allies in the fast growing towns and cities, eager for protection from local lords and happy to provide some of their wealth to the crown for protection and for charters that favored their growth. Townsmen—who just a generation or two before had been serfs—now began to amass substantial amounts of money, making the feudal system in the cities unclear. ■

Suggested Reading

Jones, *The Italian City-State from Commune to Signoria.*

Spufford, *Power and Profit.*

1. Explain why the resumption of long distance trade was the driving factor for the recovery of Europe.

2. The inheritance effect after the Black Death recapitalized European banks and trading companies, improving working conditions and wages. Do all disasters have a silver lining of some kind?

Humanism and the Italian Renaissance
Lecture 6

Feudalism put down only superficial roots in Italy. Continuing connections with the East ensured that powerful seafaring city-states sustained those elements necessary for trade. These city-states were increasingly independent from the feudal barons who ruled the rural hinterlands: They could protect themselves, administer their own justice, and extract independence by playing the power of the pope against the power of the emperor. As a result, these cities grew wealthy, especially enriched by the Crusades. This wealth created a powerful class of enormously rich merchants who governed their cities, fixed laws, and effectively became the bankers to the continent.

The Renaissance began in Italy in the 14th century and then spread somewhat unevenly over the rest of Northern Europe in the late 15th and 16th centuries. The most perfect actualization of this new culture arose in Florence. Although not a seaport, Florence had grown hugely wealthy through its production of high quality woolen cloth and banking. The newly enriched merchants found that they were thwarted in their desire to use the city government to further their ends. Moreover, the representatives of the old noble families that ruled Florence resented and despised these new men because of their lack of lineage. The result was civic tension and urban violence between the magnate families and the merchant class.

The merchants ultimately won because of their ability to cooperate, bring great wealth to bear, and generally outsmart the violent thugs of the old nobility. In 1293, the Ordinances of Justice turned Florence into a bourgeois, mercantile republic, ruled through its guild structure, intent on controlling the old families, and using the levers of government to benefit trade and commerce.

The city of Florence proved to be the natural crucible for **humanism**. In seeking a cultural model for their self definition, the merchant class turned to the Roman Republic where they saw themselves reflected. In antiquity the state was an instrument to help us here on Earth. Salvation was left to faith, as the secular and divine were separated in function. Social mobility and competition were valued, as was personal responsibility. These were the fundamental ideas that collectively came to be known as humanism. And they spawned a cultural movement that grew well beyond the borders of Florence, and, indeed, of Italy.

The city of Florence proved to be the natural crucible for humanism.

The principles of humanism became self-reinforcing and self-perpetuating. Florentines perceived themselves as different from the men of the Middle Ages, which historians described as barbarous and Gothic. Celebrated by Florentine writers like **Petrarch** and Boccaccio, the place of human values became supreme, and the Middle Ages came to define that chasm between classical antiquity and the beginning of the Italian Renaissance. Humanist values and practices spread broadly across the Italian Peninsula, as learned laymen were produced by humanist schools and sought employment in republics, monarchies, and papal Rome. Humanism proved a remarkably flexible and effective tool, setting the standards for style, scholarship, and communication, as well as art and architecture throughout Italy. ∎

Important Term

humanism: The Renaissance revival of antiquity and its application to contemporary issues.

Name to Know

Petrarch, Francesco (1304–1374): Prominent Italian poet who is commonly regarded as the father of the Italian humanism.

Suggested Reading

Brucker, *Renaissance Florence*.

Burke, *Culture and Society in Renaissance Italy*.

1. Why did the Renaissance first occur in Italy?

2. Are the values of Renaissance humanism still useful today?

Crisis in the Church
Lecture 7

There were a number of crises in the Church during the late Middle Ages, such as the Babylonian Captivity and Schism, as well as the often extortionate practices of the Church that drove many members of new social and economic groups into opposition to the established ecclesiastical order.

The Babylonian Captivity of the church began in 1309, when Pope Clement V moved the papal court to Avignon. The Great Schism began in 1378 when the leadership of the Catholic Church split under two popes, one in Rome and one in Avignon, both of whom **excommunicated** the other and named him the anti-Christ. Europe became divided over the issue with France and her allies supporting the pope in Avignon and England and her allies supporting the pope in Rome. This event was the greatest crisis in the Church up to that time and seriously undermined papal authority.

As a consequence many pious people began to look outside the Church for spiritual comfort. There was a huge increase in lay religious movements, more or less orthodox, that promised a close communion with God on a personal level, thus bypassing the institutional structure of the Church that had become so questionable.

The spread of literacy in towns and the advent of printing made the messages of heretical or popular preachers more accessible, offering a much more personal route to spiritual comfort. Groups such as the Brethren of the Common Life, from which Erasmus arose, seemed more in tune with the rise of individual conscience—personal responsibility and active spiritual life— than the sacramental model the Roman Church provided.

In Bohemia, a popular preacher, **Jan Hus** argued that the Church should not enjoy great wealth, the institutional structure was unnecessary, the Bible should be translated into the vernacular, and that each Christian should be able to approach God more directly, rather than through the mediation of a priest.

The Council of Constance in 1414 addressed the Schism and attempted to silence the Hussites, by declaring Hus a heretic and burning him at the stake. The appointment of a new pope, the widely respected Martin V Colonna, cemented the papacy once more to Rome. Nevertheless, the Babylonian Captivity and the Schism had weakened the institutional structure of the Church and the authority of the pope.

The same forces, then, that helped propel the urban intellectual, cultural, and economic experiments of the Renaissance in northern Europe contributed to the desire to free the individual spirit and experiment with new models of Church government and personal piety. The role of the pope was seriously questioned and the economic and political privileges of the Roman Church caused much anger.

It is no accident, then, that the Reformation was led by Martin Luther, an educated member of the new middle class growing ever more distant from his family's peasant origins. ■

Important Term

excommunication: The exclusion of an individual from the sacraments because of crimes against the Church or religion.

Name to Know

Hus, Jan (c. 1370–1415): Bohemian (Czech) preacher, theologian, and philosopher, Jan Hus objected to many of the practices of the Catholic Church, which he argued were not based upon scripture. Accused of heresy by the antipope John XXIII, his execution prompted the Hussite Wars (1419–1434) and the Hussite Reformation movement.

Suggested Reading

Creighton, *A History of the Papacy from the Great Schism to the Sack of Rome*.

Mollat, *The Popes at Avignon, 1305–1378*.

1. Why did the Babylonian Captivity and the Great Schism so greatly damage the Roman Church?

2. The solution to the Schism was found at the Council of Constance. Are large international conferences still useful in addressing the fundamental problems in the world?

Christian Humanism
Lecture 8

During the early Middle Ages, secular education in northern Europe had largely ceased. Even as towns grew and mercantile activity increased, learning tended to be the monopoly of the Church and scholasticism, the application of Aristotelian logic to theology, was the dominant form of teaching and learning. The intent of knowledge was in essence the justification of the ways of God to man.

Men such as **Erasmus** of Rotterdam (c. 1466–1536), who was educated by the Brethren of the Common Life, sought a devotion to pure Christianity as reflected in a simpler and more direct communication with the Church Fathers and the Apostolic Church. Through his writings, Erasmus became one of the most important voices of Christian humanism.

His most famous work, *The Praise of Folly* (1509) satirizes human frailty, particularly among clerics. In 1516, Erasmus produced his most devastating work, a Greek translation of the New Testament, correcting many errors in the standard Latin translation. Erasmus thereby challenged the hierarchy of the

© iStockphoto/Thinkstock.

Desiderius Erasmus was the most eminent humanist scholar and theologian of the Renaissance.

Church, questioning why basic Christian texts like the Bible should not be available to all believers rather than being mediated by a closed caste of priests.

Erasmus's friend **Thomas More** (1478–1535) was a humanist scholar and Lord Chancellor to Henry VIII. More's *Utopia* was the story of an imaginary island recently discovered where reason and charity are institutionalized and operate and where vanity, greed, and violence are controlled. Like Erasmus, More questioned the corruption of the clergy and the lack of charity among both secular and clerical leaders.

The work of northern Renaissance scholars like Erasmus and More was enthusiastically embraced by new groups beginning to emerge in northern cities and towns, particularly members of a growing mercantile class. This rapid spread of the ideas of the Christian humanists was directly attributable to the invention of the printing press. It was easier for more people to read the Bible, Erasmus's commentaries, as well as his and other Christian humanists' attacks on the Roman Church.

Members of the new mercantile and legal classes were educated and pious. However, they were disadvantaged by the dominance of the feudal nobility in social and political matters, and they were intellectually and culturally marginalized by the clergy. The growing tensions in the north between the old, landowning feudal nobility and the urban mercantile and legal elite provided the ideal conditions for the revolution that would come to be known as the Reformation.

External events also contributed to the psychological shock in Europe that allowed for the Reformation. The Ottomans had proven powerful and aggressive, leading to a great fear in Europe of Islam and the Turks. The voyages of discovery of Columbus and others had the unsettling effect of questioning established truths. ∎

Names to Know

Erasmus, Desiderius (c. 1466–1536): Erasmus was the most eminent humanist scholar and theologian of the Renaissance. He is known for his translation of the New Testament from the original Greek and for his literary works such as *The Praise of Folly*.

More, Thomas (1478–1535): English statesman, scholar, and writer. An uncompromising Catholic, More resigned his political office after refusing to sign the Act of Supremacy. Besides his political activity, he was one of England's leading Christian humanists, a close friend of Erasmus, and the author of one of Europe's most universally popular books, *Utopia*, published in 1516.

Suggested Reading

Nauert, *Humanism and the Culture of the Renaissance.*

Phillips, *Erasmus and the Northern Renaissance.*

Questions to Consider

1. How did the Renaissance in Northern Europe differ from the Italian Renaissance?

2. More and Erasmus believed that their societies could be improved through the practice of charity and virtue on an individual and institutional level. Is this belief applicable today?

The Ottoman Threat to Europe
Lecture 9

By the mid-14th century, the Ottoman Turk empire had become extremely powerful, conquering everything except for the rump of the erstwhile mighty Byzantine Empire. Then, in 1453, Mehmet captured Constantinople, destroying the last continuous vestige of Roman rule in the East.

Using this powerful base, **Mehmet** extended his conquests into southern Europe, capturing Venetian and Genoese trading posts in the Mediterranean. Serbia was taken in 1459, Greece in 1460, Bosnia in 1464, and Ottoman rule extended as far as the Crimea in the Black Sea. By the early 16th century, the Ottomans controlled a ring around the eastern Mediterranean that extended from the Nile to the Danube. The Mediterranean had become a Turkish lake and the Ottoman Empire was now the most powerful state in the Western world, one that had trebled in size between 1485 and 1559.

The Ottoman threat increased with the ascendancy of **Süleyman the Magnificent** (1494–1565) as sultan in 1520. Süleyman had extraordinary ambitions to conquer Latin Christendom: He first attacked the Hungarians, capturing Belgrade. In 1526, that threat increased when Süleyman's army annihilated a great Christian army led by King Louis of Hungary. In 1529, the Ottomans laid siege to Vienna, the heart of Habsburg power in the East. However, Süleyman had extended his army too far and was forced to return to the Balkans.

Nevertheless, the Ottomans remained a naval threat until 1571, when an allied Christian fleet defeated the Turks at Lepanto. Despite this victory, the Turks still controlled much of the Mediterranean and fortified their positions in eastern and southern Europe. In 1683, Vienna was once again besieged and saved only by the intervention of the king of Poland.

It is no wonder, then, that Europeans developed a great fear of Islam and the Turks, a fear that had profound effects for European society and politics, particularly on the Iberian Peninsula. Spain had long enjoyed a rich cultural and religious diversity in which Christian, Muslim, and Jewish traditions and scholarship enriched the life of the peninsula for centuries. The victories and expansion of the Ottoman Turks and the fear of Islam made this increasingly tense coexistence unsustainable. The result was that the Spanish Peninsula changed from being among the most tolerant and cosmopolitan places in Europe to one of the most intolerant.

The unification of Spain began with the dynastic union of Aragon and Castile through the marriage of Ferdinand and Isabella in 1479.

The unification of Spain began with the dynastic union of Aragon and Castile through the marriage of **Ferdinand and Isabella** in 1479. Under these fervently Catholic rulers, the Spanish Inquisition, established in 1483 and directed by Thomas de Torquemada (1420–1498) became a means of rooting out heresy and non-conformity in the realm, particularly among Muslims and Jews. A reinvigorated crusading army drove the Muslim Moors from Granada in 1492.

This triumph against the infidels in Europe gave new energy to explorers like Christopher Columbus and Vasco da Gama as they sailed to discover the New World. ■

Names to Know

Ferdinand and Isabella (1452–1516) and (1451–1504): After uniting their kingdoms in a dynastic marriage, they began a crusade to conquer those parts of Spain still under Muslim rule. The Inquisition was given great power to investigate non-Christians; within a short period of time the Iberian Peninsula changed from one of the most religiously tolerant places in Europe to among the least tolerant. It was also during their reign that Columbus discovered the New World, sailing under their flag.

Mehmet (Mohammed) the Conqueror (1432–1481): Sultan of the Ottoman Empire between 1451 and 1481. Mehmet captured Constantinople in 1453, putting an end to the Byzantine Empire. Mehmed then amalgamated the old Byzantine administration into the Ottoman state and implemented many social and educational reforms, including support for schools and universities.

Süleyman the Magnificent (1494–1566): Considered the greatest sultan of his dynasty, under his reign most of the Middle East and parts of Eastern Europe were annexed to the Ottoman Empire, as well as territories in North Africa as far as Algeria, marking the greatest extent of Ottoman rule and his empire as the most powerful in the Western world.

Suggested Reading

Reston, *Defenders of the Faith*.

Wheatcroft, *The Enemy at the Gate*.

Questions to Consider

1. Why were Europeans unable to contain the Turks?

2. Did the aggressive expansion of the Ottoman Turks into Europe and the Mediterranean begin "The Clash of Civilizations"?

The Expansion of Europe
Lecture 10

The collapse of the Italian trading monopolies in the East and the dangers of sailing Turkish waters drove Western European states to seek new trading routes. Prince Henry the Navigator, the head of a Christian crusading order who wanted to drive the Muslims from the Mediterranean, sponsored voyages farther and farther along the coast of Africa, carefully mapping and claiming territory for Portugal.

After his death, King John of Portugal sent expeditions down the coast of West Africa, increasingly close to the Cape of Good Hope. In 1488, Bartholomew Dias finally reached the tip of Africa and anchored at what is now Cape Town. In 1497–1498, Vasco da Gama succeeded in rounding the Cape and sailed up the coast of Africa, despite attacks from Muslim traders.

This venture proved that the East could be reached by circumnavigating Africa. No longer were Italian middlemen needed; and, as early as 1505, spices could be purchased in Portugal for 20 percent of the cost in Venice. As a consequence, Italy entered an economic decline as the merchants of the Atlantic seacoast took their trade and profits eastward.

The growth of the Atlantic world was encouraged and facilitated by events in Spain. Backed by Queen Isabella of Spain, **Christopher Columbus** (1451–1506) set out from Cadiz on his now famous voyage to the Indies that was interrupted by the Americas. Soon after, the Portuguese Pedro Alvares Cabral reached Brazil by accident as he was making his

Christopher Columbus's discovery of and subsequent voyages to the New World brought great riches to Spain.

way west to pick up currents that would swing him around the Cape of Good Hope.

The discovery of the Americas was to change the course of world history. Moreover, it laid the foundations for the huge Spanish Empire and provided Spain with apparently inexhaustible wealth. This allowed Spain to finance its ambitious and aggressive policies on the continent, particularly after the accession of **Charles V of Habsburg**, who would unite Spain, the Holy Roman Empire, and the Indies into the greatest power Europe had seen since Rome.

It is difficult, even in our age of space exploration, to imagine the effect that these voyages and discoveries had on the European psychology. What had been found was completely outside the collective knowledge and faith of Europeans: There is no mention of the New World in the Bible or in ancient literature, except for the vague Platonic description of Atlantis. Who were these aboriginal people, and how should they be treated?

By 1522, the Spanish began to systematically conquer the peoples in the areas they controlled. Famous conquistadors, men like **Hernando Cortes** (1485–1547) and **Francisco Pizarro** (c. 1475–1541), sought gold, glory, and the conversion of the natives they discovered to Roman Christianity.

Economic and political power and influence moved from the Mediterranean to the Atlantic seacoast and to the kingdoms north of the Alps able to take advantage of the new economy. In the 16th and 17th centuries, Spain, the Habsburg Empire, and later the Dutch Republic and England became the economic centers of Europe. Europe had been changed forever. ∎

Names to Know

Charles V of Habsburg (1500–1558): One of the most influential monarchs in the first half of the 16th century, ruling a united Spain, the Low Countries, the Empire, much of Italy, and the Indies—the greatest empire since Charlemagne. His reign was characterized by wars, particularly against the French king Francis I and against the Lutherans, as the Reformation began in Germany during his rule as Emperor.

Columbus, Christopher (1451–1506): A famous navigator and explorer, Columbus calculated that the circumference of Earth was smaller than generally believed and thought Asia could be easily reached by sailing west across the Atlantic. He convinced Isabella of Castile and Ferdinand of Aragon to support his first voyage in 1492, resulting in his discovery of the Americas. Three subsequent voyages followed, thus beginning the European conquest and colonization of the New World.

Cortes, Hernando (1485–1547): Spanish conquistador, Hernando Cortes was the leader of the expedition to Mexico that conquered the kingdom of the Aztecs.

Pizarro, Francisco (c. 1475–1541): Spanish conquistador who conquered the Incan Empire and founded Lima, the capital of Peru.

Suggested Reading

Fritze, *New Worlds*.

Pagden, *Lords of All the World*.

Questions to Consider

1. Account for the shift of the center of influence from the Mediterranean to the Atlantic seaboard.

2. What were the most powerful motives behind the voyages of discovery and the colonization of the New World?

The Continental Reformation—Luther

Lecture 11

Crisis in the Church and in European society had been developing for some time. Martin Luther was merely the most effective and visible leader of a dynamic movement, which needed structure, leadership, and justification.

As a young man, **Martin Luther** (1483–1546) had been sent to university to study law. However, a personal crisis drove him instead to enter an Augustinian priory. Despite his adherence to his vows and mortifications, Luther could not escape a sense of sin and guilt. Through study of the Bible and the Church Fathers, Luther came to believe that ceremony and good works were not the means to salvation: Faith alone was enough. Luther's belief was directly challenged in 1517 by the sale of **indulgences** in his university town of Wittenberg. To counter the idea of remission of sin for cash, Luther nailed his Ninety-Five Theses, points of disputation (theses) on the castle church door.

However, Luther's Ninety-Five Theses covered more than indulgences. He went much further, calling for the dissolution of monasteries, "a priesthood for all believers," and for a claim against the pope's authority based on the error inherent in the sale of indulgences. Luther's theses spread with astonishing speed across Germany, a movement that became known as the Reformation.

Increasingly, Luther distanced himself from Catholic orthodoxy until in 1520 he was excommunicated. By 1521, Luther had gained many supporters, particularly

Martin Luther's Ninety-Five Theses instigated the Reformation in Europe.

© Photos.com/Thinkstock.

those for whom his calls for liberty and for a priesthood for all believers resonated. Under the protection of Frederick of Saxony Luther continued to think and write, giving his new religion a coherent shape. He also undertook the translation of the Bible into German. In short, Luther institutionalized his personal revolt and founded a new church, if not a new religion.

On the other hand, Luther himself was not a social revolutionary. Indeed, during the Peasants' War of 1525 when the rebels called for his help, he called them rebels against God and recommended their slaughter. Luther needed the princes and nobles of Germany to effect his revolution, so he saw these powerful men as God's ministers and argued that Church property and law should be under the control of secular rulers.

By 1529, Germany was divided almost in half between the Catholics and Lutherans and in 1531 this division took the form of a military alliance. Wars and battles followed but neither side could triumph. In 1555 at the Diet of Augsburg it was agreed that the religion of the prince would decide the religion of his subjects. Some measure of peace resulted.

Luther's revolt had destroyed forever the unity of the Church, encouraging other reformers, such as **Ulrich Zwingli** (1484–1531) of Zurich. Although Zwingli was killed in 1531 in an early war of religion, his brand of reform sowed the seeds for the emergence of John Calvin. Once the breach was opened, a number of other religious leaders, each preaching a different doctrine, challenged Lutheranism and Catholicism and the very souls of Europeans. ■

Important Term

indulgences: The documents available for purchase from the Church in order to accelerate the release of souls from purgatory.

Luther, Martin (1483–1546): German monk, theologian, instigator of the European Reformation, and founder of Lutheranism. In 1517, Luther nailed his Ninety-Five Theses to the Castle Church door in Wittenberg to challenge the sale of indulgencies, claiming that salvation is a gift from God received by grace through faith in Christ. His personal revolt resulted in the division of Christendom into many, often warring sects, a situation that would lead to over a century of bloodshed.

Zwingli, Ulrich (1484–1531): Preacher in Zurich and a leader of the Swiss Reformation, Zwingli attacked ecclesiastical abuses, advocated priestly marriage, and disputed Catholic dogma of the presence of Christ in the Eucharist. This brought him into conflict with other reformers, notably Luther.

Suggested Reading

Bainton, *Here I Stand: A Life of Martin Luther*.

MacCulloch, *The Reformation*.

Questions to Consider

1. Account for the success of the Lutheran revolt.

2. Why did the reformed confessions splinter into a number of mutually exclusive warring sects after Luther's break with Rome?

The Continental Reformation—Calvin
Lecture 12

Once the breach with Catholicism was established, other reformers such as the Swiss priest and scholar of Christian humanism, Ulrich Zwingli, emerged to challenge the Roman and Lutheran Confessions. Zwingli was a major influence on John Calvin, the most important of the second generation of reformers.

A Frenchman trained in the law, **John Calvin** (1509–1564) adopted reformed beliefs and was consequently driven into exile. In 1536 he entered Geneva whose reformation and society he would direct until the end of his days. *The Institutes of the Christian Religion*, his book which he elaborated throughout his life, became a necessary text for understanding Calvin's mind and his control of the city.

For Calvin, God was a distant, angry figure who demanded moral accommodation imposed on Geneva's citizens by a lay consistory with the power to excommunicate and correct. Calvin argued that because God is omniscient and omnipotent, He knew from the beginning of time who was reprobate and who was saved. Consequently, there was nothing an individual could do to save him or herself.

Yet despite this foreordained destiny, Calvin insisted that everyone—even the damned—should be forced to lead lives that would be pleasing to God. Much art, secular music, dancing, cards, and other simple pleasures were banned in this theocracy created by Calvin.

Although rigorous, Calvin's message was strong and popular. In the confused spiritual world of the Reformation, people were looking for a straight, clear answer, and Calvin provided this. He also organized Calvinism into independent cells that could set down roots anywhere and spread the Word. Printing presses and a university in Geneva sent tracts and missionaries to expand the religion.

The result was that by the time of Calvin's death in 1564, France, too, had been divided almost in half between **Huguenots** and Catholics. His word also spread to the Low Countries.

The impact of Calvinism in France would have devastating results. Most importantly, Calvinism led directly to the Wars of Religion in 1562 and the St. Bartholomew's Day Massacre of 1572. The revolution that Luther began and Zwingli and Calvin extended resulted in over a century of vicious and constant warfare. These wars that appeared to be about minor points of theology, but in fact reflected the fundamental social, political, and economic shifts on the continent for which religion provided the only accepted vocabulary of change and reconstruction.

John Calvin's theological work influenced the development of several branches of Protestantism.

Europe was now fragmented into a great many churches—in fact, religions—at war with one another, often despite only minor doctrinal differences. With Luther, the property and jurisdiction of the Roman Church were usurped by secular authorities. With Calvin, even consciences belonged to the state, which had the duty to impose its will not only on what its citizens did and said but also on what they thought. ∎

Important Term

Huguenot: A French Protestant, usually a Calvinist.

Calvin, John (1509–1564): A pastor and theologian, Calvin published his seminal theological work, *Institutes of the Christian Religion* in 1536. In this work Calvin developed his doctrine of predestination and salvation by the grace of God. Calvin's thought directly influenced the development of several branches of Protestantism, such as Puritanism and Presbyterianism.

Suggested Reading

Bouwsma, *A Sixteenth-Century Portrait.*

Gordon, *The Swiss Reformation.*

Questions to Consider

1. Why was Calvin's message so attractive to so many Europeans?

2. The Protestant Reformation was spread by the printing press. Can you identify other challenges to authority dependent on new technology?

The Wars of Religion
Lecture 13

The Catholic Church had been attacked by Luther, Zwingli, Calvin, and eventually Henry VIII of England, destroying forever the unity of Christendom. The Church was not prepared to accept the loss of so many adherents and consequently sought to respond to the Protestant challenge. Under the brilliant leadership of Pope Paul III the Roman Church addressed the challenges of Protestant revolutionaries through the great Council of Trent.

In the years of its deliberations, 1545–1563, the Council of Trent redefined and reinforced Catholic doctrine and hierarchy, largely rejecting Protestant demands. The Latin Vulgate Bible was affirmed as the true source of scripture. St. Thomas Aquinas, the 13th-century scholastic theologian, was adopted as the central thinker for the shaping of Catholic dogma. The central authority of the pope was maintained, the seven sacraments were upheld, and saints were still recognized. The centrally managed Roman Inquisition was sustained to identify heresy; and, in 1559, the **Index of Prohibited Books** was decreed to control heretical ideas.

Simultaneously a new zeal took hold of the Church. Just as the Council of Trent clarified and reinforced the faith of Catholics, the foundation of the Jesuit Order by **Ignatius of Loyola** provided the instrument by which that faith would be affirmed, taught, and spread. These priests were to live among the people, engaging in teaching, preaching, and missionary activity. The natives of the New World were to be converted to Roman Christianity and souls both protected and won back from the Protestants in Europe.

The spirit that brought about the Jesuits also brought about the religious wars of the 16th and 17th centuries. The Jesuits and their superb schools, together with the Inquisition and the Index, represented a different kind of religious war: a war of the spirit and of will between Protestants and Catholics. Europe had been divided by religion, and the ultimate consequence of this was a century of unspeakable suffering.

In particular, confessional allegiance was tearing apart France, where Calvinism had spread rapidly. France was slowly being broken into two kingdoms: one Roman Catholic and one Calvinist led by the Bourbons. In 1559, a lengthy and brutal civil war broke out.

By the1580s, under a weak king, the Guise family had grown increasingly powerful, forming the Catholic League to keep the Huguenot Henri de Bourbon from inheriting the throne. But despite their alliance with Spain, a series of intrigues and assassinations led to an unexpected reversal, with the Protestant **Henri IV** becoming king of France in 1589.

In a deft political maneuver, Henri IV converted to Catholicism; and in 1593, he united the country in

Ignatius of Loyola founded the Society of Jesus, or the Jesuit Order.

© Photos.com/Thinkstock.

a war against Spain. After the peace in 1598, he cemented the religious reconciliation with the celebrated Edict of Nantes, granting toleration and full civil rights to Huguenots. But this policy of rational compromise could not protect Henri himself: He was assassinated in 1610 by a Catholic fanatic. ■

Index of Prohibited Books: Books which Catholics were prohibited from reading or possessing, first established in 1559.

Names to Know

Henri IV of France (1553–1610): Also Henry of Navarre, King Henri IV effectively ended the French Wars of Religion (1562–1598). He was one of the most popular and successful monarchs of his age, unusually tolerant and concerned for the welfare of his people. He followed practical political advice from his advisers, who put the well-being of his kingdom above all other considerations, including religion.

Loyola, Ignatius of (1491–1556): Ignatius of Loyola was a Spanish soldier who in 1521 underwent a religious conversion, subsequently becoming a hermit and a priest. In 1540, Loyola founded the Society of Jesus, or the Jesuit Order. It was largely as a result of the work of the Jesuits that Catholicism was able to withstand the attacks of the Protestants, return many to the Roman confession, and convert the inhabitants of newly contacted lands to the Catholic religion.

Suggested Reading

Holt, *The French Wars of Religion, 1562–1629*.

O'Malley, *Trent and All That*.

Questions to Consider

1. Why did the reformation of the Church lead to a century of terrible war and bloodshed?

2. Henri IV, on the advice of *les politiques*, issued the tolerant Edict of Nantes. Can you suggest why it took until 1598 to experiment with the principle of religious toleration?

Lecture 13: The Wars of Religion

The English Reformation
Lecture 14

While the continental Reformation and wars of religion fragmented European society, England embarked upon a royal reformation of the Church, which would in the fullness of time breed the seeds of its own religious wars.

By the early 16th century religious discontent was already on the rise. The vast wealth and luxury of the monasteries, the ungodly behavior of many clerics, the rise of Lutheranism in Germany, and the criticism of monasticism by Thomas More and Erasmus encouraged negative thinking about the Church. Anticlericalism became widespread, and many powerful local lords began to demand parts of the large tracts of Church lands.

As late as the 1520s, England had remained loyal to Rome. But in 1527, with no prospect of a male heir from his marriage to Catherine of Aragon, **Henry VIII** (1491–1547) petitioned the pope for a divorce. When the pope refused, Henry turned to Parliament and the Archbishop of Canterbury to declare the marriage void. In the process, Parliament began dismantling the Roman Church in England and transferring its jurisdiction and property to the crown, most famously through the dissolution of the monasteries. Henry was declared supreme head of the Church in England, and the authority of the pope was denied.

© Photos.com/Thinkstock.

Henry VIII set in motion a chain of events that led to England's break with Catholicism when the pope refused to annul his marriage.

Henry himself remained theologically conservative and insisted that most Catholic beliefs and practices continue despite urgings from many around him for reform. But when his son, Edward (1547–1553), assumed the throne on Henry's death, Edward's councilors and parliaments introduced legislation that brought the English Church more into line with continental Protestantism as represented in the *Book of Common Prayer* (1549) and the *Act of Uniformity* (1552), which abandoned Catholic mass and allowed clerical marriage.

Edward was succeeded by his older half sister, Mary. A devout Catholic, Mary briefly brought an end to the Protestant Reformation, reconciling the English Church with Rome in 1554. Mass was once again heard in English churches, altars returned, and crosses reappeared. But her unpopular marriage to **Philip II of Spain** (1527–1598) in 1554 was childless, allowing her Protestant half sister, Elizabeth, to take the throne in 1558.

Elizabeth I (1533–1603) returned to the church of her father but in doctrine her Established Church was closer in practice to Calvin than to the pope. Initially Elizabeth was willing to allow Catholics to practice their religion in private. However, this clemency changed when the pope declared Elizabeth a heretic and called upon her subjects to rebel against the queen. Elizabeth's hostility to Catholics grew more stringent after a series of plots against her rule.

Most famously, she executed her Catholic cousin, Mary, Queen of Scots, because of constant plotting. This resulted in the failed Spanish Armada of 1588 led by Philip of Spain. After this, England was secure at home and actively engaged on the Continent against Spain and other Catholic powers. Nevertheless, the problem of the religious reform continued to fester, and would eventually lead to civil war and regicide. ■

Elizabeth I, the last monarch of the Tudor dynasty.

Elizabeth I of England (1533–1603): The last monarch of the Tudor dynasty, she succeeded Mary I on the throne ending a decade of political and religious turmoil. During Elizabeth I's reign sensitive and pragmatic policies in religion were implemented; England grew as a naval and imperial power, defeating the Spanish Armada in 1588 and staking claim to the future British colonies in North America and the Caribbean; and England experienced a great cultural richness by establishing the Elizabethan Age.

Henry VIII of England (1491–1547): At the beginning of his reign Henry VIII was described as an ideal Renaissance prince but soon fell into despair at his failure to secure a male heir. Henry struggled to annul his first marriage by seeking papal approval through the intercession of his chief minister, Cardinal Wolsey. When the pope did not grant an annulment, Henry set in motion a chain of events that led to England's break with Catholicism and to the consummation of his short-lived marriage to Anne Boleyn. This marriage, which produced a daughter, Elizabeth, ended with Anne's beheading in 1536. Four more marriages followed, the third of which, to Jane Seymour, produced the desired male heir, the future Edward VI.

Philip II of Spain (1527–1598): Son and co-heir of Charles V of Habsburg, the Holy Roman Emperor. Philip inherited his father's leadership of the Catholic cause in Europe, warring against the Calvinists in the Netherlands and sending the Armada against England in 1588. He benefited from the rich treasures coming from the Spanish dominions in the New World and sustained, as a result, a vigorous foreign and military policy.

Suggested Reading

Duffy, *The Stripping of the Altars*.

Haigh, English Reformations.

1. How did the reformation in England differ from the reformations on the Continent?

2. The English Reformation has been described as "faith by statute." Can or should the state legislate religious observance or conformity?

The English Civil War
Lecture 15

During Elizabeth's reign, the House of Commons had begun to increasingly challenge the nobles for political power. As nobles were expected to live at court, rural land owners, whose estates varied from small holdings to vast landed wealth, took over their traditional roles in the provinces, most significantly as members of Parliament. As such, they increasingly saw themselves as vital to the political future of the kingdom, particularly in matters of taxation, religion, and foreign policy.

When Queen Elizabeth died without heirs in 1603, she was succeeded by James I, the son of Mary, Queen of Scots. James I had little experience of English affairs. In order to keep the peace, he permitted the House of Commons to whittle away at the royal prerogative, merely emboldening the religious radicals in Parliament—the **Puritans**.

In 1625, James was succeeded by his son **Charles I** (1600–1649). Charles soured his reign at the beginning first by agreeing to The Petition of Right in order to get a tax subsidy and then by trying to repudiate it. Parliament was furious, so Charles dissolved the house and ruled without Parliament from 1629–1640.

But Charles's confused religious policy alienated his other kingdom, Scotland, when he tried to impose an Anglican prayer book on the Presbyterian Scots. The Scots rebelled, invading northern England. Charles summoned Parliament to levy taxes for an army, but the commons demanded first that their grievances against him be heard.

Tensions soon developed into open civil war in 1641, as Charles attempted to arrest the parliamentary leaders of the Puritan opposition to his rule. This attack on the privileges of Parliament drove the commons to support the Scots and raise an army to defeat the king. Initially the war was a stalemate, until the parliamentarians reorganized their forces into the New Model Army under **Oliver Cromwell** (1599–1658), defeating Charles in 1645.

Religious moderates felt that Charles' tendency to absolute rule had been smashed; but the radicals disagreed. So a new civil war broke out, resulting in Cromwell's victory and Charles' beheading in 1649. The House of Lords was abolished, all moderates were expelled from Parliament, and Cromwell ruled as a dictator until his death in 1658.

The Teaching Company Collection.

The Stuarts were briefly restored to the throne in 1660. But their Catholic practices together with a tendency to absolutist rule led a group of influential peers and merchants to invite William of Orange from Holland to assume the throne in 1688.

William and Mary took the throne in a bloodless revolution, ever since known as the Glorious

A talented strategist and military innovator, Oliver Cromwell led the anti-royalist coalition in the English Civil War against King Charles I.

Revolution. Under him emerged a new Protestant regime that enjoyed the support of most of the kingdom and ensured the end to civil war. Parliament ruled that no Catholic could ever assume the English crown. It had taken a second revolution to complete the work of the first. ■

Puritans: The general term for English reformers who wished a complete break from Roman Catholic liturgy, practice, and symbols in the later 16th and 17th centuries.

Charles I of England (1600–1649): Provoked the English Civil Wars (1642–1649) with his marriage to the Catholic Henrietta Maria of France, sympathy with conservative Anglican practices and theology, and his high-handed dealing with Parliament. Defeated in his campaigns against the forces of the Parliament, Charles was arrested, charged with high treason, and executed. His execution prompted the temporary abolition of the monarchy in England and the institution of the Commonwealth during the Interregnum.

Cromwell, Oliver (1599–1658): A talented strategist and military innovator, he led the anti-royalist coalition in the English Civil War against King Charles I. After the execution of Charles, Cromwell presided over the Commonwealth of England and was awarded by Parliament the title of Lord Protector. Ruling with no constitutional authority, effectively as military dictator, Cromwell expelled his critics from Parliament, abolished the House of Lords, and instituted a strict Puritan regime.

Suggested Reading

Adamson, *The Noble Revolt.*

Braddick, *God's Fury, England's Fire.*

1. Was the English Civil War about religion or power?

2. Was the restoration of the monarchy under Charles I's son, Charles II, the only possible way to return England to stability?

The Thirty Years' War
Lecture 16

The Thirty Years' War (1618–1648) was perhaps the most terrible of the internal wars of religion that ravaged Europe in the 16th and 17th centuries. Its crucible was Bohemia, one of the crowns attached to the Habsburg Holy Roman Empire. There had been wide toleration of Protestants in Bohemia early in the 17th century, but in 1617 a zealous fanatic, Ferdinand, assumed the crown, intent on making Bohemia uniformly Catholic.

Refusing to accept this, the Bohemians declared Ferdinand deposed and invited the Protestant German prince Frederick, to be their king. As a consequence, Ferdinand made war on the Bohemians. Supported by other Catholic powers and the Spanish branch of the Habsburgs, he secured a total victory in 1620, after which Protestant nobles were exiled or executed and their lands given to Catholics.

This success frightened the Protestant powers of Europe and emboldened the Catholics. Ferdinand, zealot that he was, wanted to destroy the Reformation altogether, so in 1629 he issued the sweeping Edict of Restitution, which required that all Catholic Church property taken since 1555 be returned. This act galvanized all the Protestant powers and their populations against the empire.

Sweden then assumed the leadership of the Protestant cause, subsidized by French money. Led by King **Gustavus Adolfus** (1594–1632), it was initially successful in its attacks on the Habsburgs, but Gustavus was killed at the battle of Lutzen in 1632. In a tactical maneuver, Ferdinand, himself also weakened, tried to rally the empire behind him by rescinding the Edict of Restitution. But by now the French had become deeply involved, particularly against the Spanish, whom they defeated in 1643.

The Thirty Years' War had devastated Europe. It had involved almost the entire continent from Scandinavia to Poland to Portugal to Italy. Weary of fighting, and with the emperor Ferdinand dead in 1637, the major powers met for almost four years in southern Germany before the signing the Treaty of Westphalia (1648), which was to establish the foundations of European state relations for the next 150 years until the Congress of Vienna.

The Europe that emerged from the Thirty Years' War was a very different place. The German religious and political situation was settled and local princes gained more autonomy over their affairs, including taxation, defense, and legislation. Religious issues had been superseded by dynastic, political and strategic concerns: Never again would Europe divide into

© Photos.com/Thinkstock.

A talented diplomat and general, King Gustavus Adolfus was able to make Sweden one of the most powerful states in the world during his reign from 1611–1632.

warring camps over religion. France emerged as the most powerful state on the continent, eclipsing Spain and the empire, which were now poorer and in decline.

The long years of war had seen a transformation of Europe, creating the basic institutions of the modern political landscape, the notion of territorial sovereignty, the establishment of centralized government and bureaucratic administration, permanent standing armies, a secular state, and the international system of diplomacy. ■

Gustavus Adolfus of Sweden (1594–1632): King of Sweden from 1611–1632. A talented diplomat and general, he was able to make Sweden one of the most powerful states in the world. During the Thirty Years War, he became the leader of the Protestant alliance against the Catholic Habsburgs and waged successful campaigns against them until confronted by the imperial army under Wallenstein. Besides his reputation as a soldier and devout Protestant monarch, he was a supporter of the arts, science, and culture, founding the University of Uppsala.

Suggested Reading

Parker, *The Thirty Years' War*.

Wilson, *The Thirty Years War*.

Questions to Consider

1. Why was the Thirty Years War such a long, Europe-wide conflict?

2. The Peace of Westphalia was the first great multilateral conference to address complex continental problems. Why was this the only mechanism possible to end the conflict?

The Absolute Monarchy
Lecture 17

> The Reformation, the Wars of Religion, and the Civil Wars of the 16th and 17th centuries drove Europeans to seek theoretical explanations for the disintegration of traditional society and offer remedies that would provide security and stability. The chaos and anxiety of those times fostered a retreat into absolutism—regimes in which monarchs rule without restraint from any other agency.

English philosopher **Thomas Hobbes**'s treatise, *Leviathan* (1651), provided a theoretical justification for absolutism, arguing that in a state of nature the strong preyed on the weak until a contract was made in which all subjects relinquished their rights to a king who, with his successors, would enjoy in perpetuity complete power over his subjects. According to Hobbes, even if a king proved to be cruel or tyrannical, this bargain could not be undone, as only an absolute monarch could control the chaos that had existed in man's natural state.

Absolutism first developed successfully in France under Louis XIII (r. 1610–1643) under the guidance of **Cardinal Richelieu** (1619–1683). In his desire to raise the authority of Louis above the traditional privileges of the nobility, the divisive practices of the Huguenots, and the threats from France's enemies, Richelieu crafted a state in which the authority of the king could not be challenged and all resources of the kingdom were at his command.

However, Richelieu's death in the same year as Louis XIII's resulted in this system collapsing, for the new king, **Louis XIV** (r. 1643–1715), was only five years old. Civil Wars followed, driven by nobles and the Parlement of Paris trying to regain their privileges and abetted by foreign powers eager to weaken France. But by 1661, Louis XIV had assumed complete authority.

Louis XIV's powerful minister of finance, **Jean-Baptiste Colbert** (1619–1683), was an administrative genius who transformed the French economy. Under Colbert, glory, style, victory, and wealth seemed to reside in France at the court of the Sun King Louis XIV. Colbert protected

French manufacturing and agriculture and greatly strengthened the navy and merchant fleets, supporting colonial expansion. He financed Louis's building of the Palace of Versailles, beginning in 1668. The huge palace became not only the symbol of royal absolutism, but also its instrument as it served to control the nobility.

But the second half of Louis XIV's reign saw a much less glorious time. In response to French military success, other powers on the continent formed overwhelming alliances against France, resulting in almost constant war that drained the French treasury. In

With the help of able ministers, Louis XIV perfected the practice of absolute monarchy, making the crown independent of any control.

some ways, Louis XIV's greatest failure of leadership was the revocation of the Edict of Nantes in 1685, declaring Protestantism illegal and driving almost 200,000 of his most useful citizens abroad, most into the states of his enemies.

Still, France managed to sustain its position as a great power. When Louis died in 1715, the world he represented was being challenged by ideas hostile to his political absolutism and religious **obscurantism**. ■

obscurantism: Opposition to free enquiry, rationalism, and the Enlightenment, in particular..

parlement: French law courts in major cities before the Revolution, with the Parlement of Paris having extraordinary authority and respect.

Names to Know

Colbert, Jean-Baptiste (1619–1683): The most prominent minister under Louis XIV, Colbert regulated imports, exports, and trade, centralizing economic activity. Under his system, France built a great navy and merchant fleet and facilitated the structure of absolutism through centralized policies at court. However, the French economy, both mercantile and agricultural, ultimately suffered from over-regulation and high taxation.

Hobbes, Thomas (1588–1679): English political theorist and scientist. In 1651 he published *Leviathan*, which postulated a secular notion of sovereignty based on a contract between ruler and subjects. Hobbes sought obscurity, although his book was to influence subsequent political thought greatly, inspiring Locke and Rousseau to respond to his theory of contract later in his century and the next.

Louis XIV of France (1638–1715): With the help of able ministers, Louis XIV perfected the practice of absolute monarchy, making the crown independent of any control. His reign, particularly the first half, reflected the economic, military, and cultural dominance of France on the Continent. His expenditures and his conduct of almost incessant wars eventually drained the treasury and exposed the crown to serious debt. Nevertheless, his reign represented a Golden Age of French influence in culture and manufacturing.

Richelieu, Cardinal Armand-Jean de (1585–1642): French cleric and statesman who rose to power during the reign of Louis XIII. While serving as a Secretary of State, Richelieu was ruthless in his building of absolutism, paying little attention to the suffering of the poor or the rights of organizations outside the crown. He humbled the nobility and replaced them in the provinces with royal intendants and he weakened the powers of the French *parlements*. He was tolerant in religion, however, reissuing the edict of Nantes and showing generosity to the Huguenots.

Suggested Reading

Bercé, *The Birth of Absolutism*.

Bergin, *Cardinal Richelieu*.

Questions to Consider

1. How was Richelieu able to effect an absolute monarchy in France?

2. Discuss how the regime of Louis XIV illustrated the strengths and weaknesses in absolute rule.

The Scientific Revolution
Lecture 18

The Scientific Revolution's two great instigators were the Englishman **Francis Bacon** (1561–1626) and the Frenchman **René Descartes** (1596–1650). They both asked the question: How can we make true observations and conclusions about man and nature? Bacon in *Novum Organum* (1620) argued that all things must be held as possible until tested, while Descartes in his *Discourse on Method* (1637) suggested accepting anything as certain only if verified objectively.

Francis Bacon, English philosopher best known for his work *Novum Organum*.

Galileo Galilei (1564–1642) advanced the principle of experimental science. He developed hypotheses and tested his assumptions experimentally, building a telescope to observe the heavens and famously challenging the Roman Church's teachings about the placement of Earth in the solar system. Each of these men started with a concept of doubt, refusing to accept anything as true until proven. The result was the intellectual and political revolutions of the 18th century, animated by the primacy of reason and the relegation of faith to a subservient sphere.

Isaac Newton (1643–1727) and **John Locke** (1632–1704) perpetuated this intellectual revolution. Newton developed calculus and combined physics and astronomy to create the modern conception of the immutable forces that move the universe—gravity, inertia, weight, mass, and motion. The great work which put Newton on the European landscape of intellectual luminaries was *Principia Mathematica* or *Mathematical Principles* (1687). God in the Newtonian universe becomes passive and distant: If God exists at all, it is as the inventor, the force who set the pendulum swinging. So, if God is not needed to operate the universe, perhaps He also leaves us alone on Earth to run our own affairs.

Isaac Newton, English mathematician.

Also influenced by the power of science and reasoning, John Locke was a theorist of government and rational understanding who used **empiricism** to promote concepts of human dignity and inalienable human rights. Locke was trained in medicine, natural philosophy, rhetoric, and classical literature. In his *Essay on Human Understanding* (completed 1666, published 1690), Locke posited a theory of man as tabula rasa, a blank slate at birth, which is progressively filled through sense experience.

John Locke, political theorist and founder of empiricism.

Locke applied these notions to politics in his *Second Treatise on Government* (1690). He argued that despite the differences in human experience, all men had reason, and that reason impelled them to form a contract between governor and governed. Unlike Hobbes, Locke didn't believe these governments would be based on restraint. For Locke, absolute government was inherently inconsistent with a civil society and human dignity.

Instead, governments were formed to protect man's natural rights: the rights to life, liberty, and property, rights that could not be alienated without their express consent. ∎

Important Term

empiricism: The scientific and philosophical system based upon the assessment and recognition of verifiable, observable evidence and sense experience to determine knowledge.

Names to Know

Bacon, Francis (1561–1626): English philosopher, historian, founder of empirical science, and politician. Bacon is best known for the method of scientific inquiry called induction, which is the acquisition of knowledge through experimentation and observation, described in *Novum Organum* (1620).

Descartes, René (1596–1650): Key figure in the scientific revolution, with important contributions in the fields of mathematics and philosophy. In mathematics, he invented the Cartesian coordinate system, which allows functions to be expressed as algebraic equations. His short treatise of 1637, *The Discourse on Method*, defined scientific method and institutionalized the principle that phenomena had to be proven true before being accepted. In philosophy the method of radical skepticism was first formulated in his *Principles of Philosophy* (1644).

Galilei, Galileo (1564–1642): Italian physicist, astronomer, philosopher, and mathematician, Galileo Galilei is recognized today as a founder of modern science. He invented and used a telescope to observe the Moon, planets, and stars, making a series of important scientific discoveries. Galileo was also the inventor of experiential physics, replacing the speculative metaphysics of Aristotle and building the foundation for mechanics.

Locke, John (1632–1704): English educator, political theorist, and a founder of empiricism. Locke argued that human beings are born without any inborn knowledge (*tabula rasa*) and knowledge is acquired through sense experience, which can be structured and taught to all children. Differences among men, then, were the result of varying education and experience, rather than intrinsic qualities of birth. Although written in part as a response to the Glorious Revolution, his *Second Treatise of Civil Government*, which argued that all humans are born with inalienable rights to life, liberty, and happiness, soon became a fundamental statement of Liberal principle.

Newton, Isaac (1643–1727): Greatest English mathematician of his generation, Newton laid the foundation for differential and integral calculus, and his work on optics and gravitation made him one of the greatest scientists the world has ever known. Newton established science as the method for addressing the problems of nature and thus, by extension, mankind.

Suggested Reading

Dear, *Revolutionizing the Sciences*.

Henry, *The Scientific Revolution and the Origins of Modern Science*.

Questions to Consider

1. Why was the codification of scientific method so central to the development of Europe?

2. Is it fair to speak of a pre- and post-Cartesian world?

The Enlightenment, Part 1
Lecture 19

The Enlightenment, or Age of Reason, can be seen as commencing with the publication of Descartes's *Discourse on Method* (1637) and ending with the Romantic movement that characterized the end of the 18th century and the beginning of the 19th century. The Enlightenment was hostile to the irrational, whether in religion or politics, and sought freedom, progress, and knowledge of the natural world through the critical use of reason.

After Galileo and Newton had proven the absolute, universal laws of nature, there developed a growing belief that nature itself could be understood and ultimately controlled. And if the universe is a great, complex machine ticking away with no divine interference, and if the principles that drive that machine are understood, then it follows that rational men and women can alter those circumstances within their control, such as their political, social, and economic systems.

French writer, Voltaire was one of the leaders of the Enlightenment.

One of the great voices of reason in France was **Voltaire** (1694–1778). Through his serious writings he popularized the work of Newton and Locke, and through his witty satire—such as *Candide*—he revealed the absurdities and failures of absolutist regimes. Despite his hostility to the Church, Voltaire was not an atheist but a **deist**, one who believed in God and an operative morality stemming from human reason that did not require divine revelation or ecclesiastical order. For Voltaire, all men had to do was rely on their reason and most of the problems of evil would diminish, if not outright disappear. For him, man was self-sufficient on Earth and the problem of any afterlife was irrelevant.

© Photos.com/Thinkstock.

It was **Baron de Montesquieu** (1689–1755) who provided the political mechanism for implementing Enlightenment theory through the publication of *The Spirit of the Laws* (1748). In it, he argued for a secular society in which the traditions of a nation, together with such contextual items as geography and climate, determined the nature of the state. Consequently, society had to be pluralistic: no single force could ever be strong enough to suppress completely the others operating simultaneously. This would be tyranny and clearly contrary to the dictates of nature and reason.

Montequieu's model was England where the separation of powers and natural checks and balances resulted in citizens being secure in their lives, liberty, and property. Indeed, Montesquieu is heavily dependent on Locke, supplemented by his own observations of the English political and social system. What Montesquieu liked about Britain was its mixed government of monarchy, aristocracy, and democracy. Like Newton's laws of motion, such a constitution did not need monitoring, because each group, seeking its own rational self-interest, checked the others, thus ensuring freedom for all; and Montesquieu wished some similar method of governance for France.

Montesquieu's great book, *The Spirit of the Laws*, offered a rational, practical alternative, one so appealing that it informed the drafters of the Constitution of the United and States and guided the early debates of the revolution in France. ∎

Important Term

deism: A belief in a supreme being as first cause in the creation of a rational universe but with no fixed ecclesiastical or theological structure.

Names to Know

Montesquieu, Charles de Secondat, Baron de (1689–1755): French political thinker of the Enlightenment who articulated the theory of the separation of powers. He proposed that the monarchy, the aristocracy, and the commons operate as mutual checks and balances augmented by the existence of an independent judiciary and administrative structure. A powerful opponent of the ancien régime, he believed that absolutism was unnatural since it failed to allow for authorities outside the crown and could not respond to local traditions.

Voltaire (1694–1778): Famous French man of letters and one of the leaders of the Enlightenment. He possessed a caustic wit and keen powers of observation and ridicule, which caused him both to be arrested and patronized. Perhaps Voltaire's greatest contribution was in the popularization of the central ideas of the Enlightenment through his witty books, entries in the *Encyclopédie,* and copious correspondence.

Suggested Reading

Pangle, *Montesquieu's Philosophy of Liberalism.*

Outram, *The Enlightenment.*

Voltaire, *Candide and Other Stories.*

Questions to Consider

1. How did Voltaire popularize and spread the ideas of the Enlightenment?

2. Discuss the influence of Montesquieu's *The Spirit of the Laws* on the Constitution of the United States.

The Enlightenment, Part 2
Lecture 20

There were other intellectuals besides Voltaire and Montesquieu who challenged the political and religious authorities in 18th-century France, and of these Denis Diderot was among the most influential.

Greatley influenced by English Enlightenment thinkers, **Denis Diderot** (1713–1784) argued for a more humane political and religious order. He followed Voltaire in attacking Christianity and the Roman Catholic Church, arguing that religions based on supernatural revelation were unnatural, anti-social, irrational, and therefore dangerous. And he argued that the same kind of irrational thought was evident in nationalism and absolutism.

It was in part to make accessible the information needed for enlightened public debate that Denis Diderot and his associates conspired to amass all knowledge into one enormous publication, the *Encyclopédie*. Between 1751 and 1772, this massive work of scholarship and propaganda appeared in 28 volumes of text and illustrations. The goal was to change the general mode of thinking. The idea of science as progress entered the Western consciousness widely through the *Encyclopédie*. Through its volumes, ordinary Frenchmen in the provinces could access the thought of Parisian luminaries of the Enlightenment. Moreover, it was self-consciously critical of every received opinion and established institution: All knowledge had to be

French writer and philosopher, Denis Diderot's greatest contribution was his work on the *Encyclopédie*.

reviewed and criticized. The purpose of the *Encyclopédie* was, by definition, revolutionary.

But perhaps the most radical thinker of the Enlightenment was Jean-Jacques Rousseau (1712–1778) whose text, *The Social Contract* (1762), was to become the bible of the French Revolution. Rousseau used the same principle of a contract between governor and governed that informed the work of Hobbes and Locke; but he turned it on its head. He argued that man in a state of nature was good and that individuals surrendered freely all their rights, not to a king, but to the community as a whole. The dignity of mankind and the operation of reason ensure that the decisions of the general will are good and act for the welfare of the whole.

The idea of science as progress entered the Western consciousness widely through the *Encyclopédie*.

By empowering the people at large, Rousseau offered a dramatic shift of authority within the state and legitimized ideas that previously had enjoyed little support. And, by suggesting that simple people, without education or cultivation, were superior because they were closer to their natural, virtuous selves, Rousseau was challenging the very concept of society itself.

However, Rousseau argued that this contract could only be seen to work before a people had been tainted by civilization. For him, France was too large and corrupt to enjoy any of the primitive virtue which is required for the formation of this general, sovereign will. The only hope was for the arrival of a great lawgiver to restore the dignity of the people. For a nation about to begin a revolution, such ideas were dynamite, and Rousseau became the favorite ideologue of the Revolution that broke out a decade following his death, a Revolution that sought to rebuild French society, partly in the image Rousseau designed. ■

Diderot, Denis (1713–1784): French writer, philosopher, art critic, and playwright. Diderot is known for his important contributions to literature and letters, but his editing of the great *Encyclopédie* with Jean d'Alembert is his greatest contribution to the mind of Europe. He wrote over 1,000 entries personally and assigned many others to the greatest experts of his day. He believed powerfully in the centrality of free speech and a free press to disseminate correct information for rational, enlightened action in every aspect of life.

Suggested Reading

Blom, *Enlightening the World.*

Ritter, *Jean-Jacques Rousseau's Political Writings.*

Questions to Consider

1. Do you agree with Diderot's claim that freedom of speech and reliable information to inform it were the fundamental platform on which a free society was built?

2. Rousseau has been described both as the architect of the principle of popular sovereignty and as the precursor of totalitarianism. What is your opinion?

France in 1789
Lecture 21

On the eve of the Revolution, French society remained an anachronism. Its population was still divided legally into the three estates of clergy, nobility, and people. The clergy were the smallest in number; yet they controlled vast estates which were exempt from taxation.

Almost all the higher appointments in the Church remained the privilege of the nobility who were greater in number and controlled nearly a quarter of the land of France—one third, if royal estates were included. The great families lived at Versailles, gaining unfair benefit from the crown, while poorer nobles remained in the provinces, squeezing rent from their tenants.

The third estate of the people represented 95 percent of the population, ranging from hugely wealthy bankers to desperately poor, landless laborers. All taxes fell on this class, especially the rural peasants. Not surprisingly, educated urban professionals called for reform. King Louis XVI was a good man but he was weak of will and hampered by a meddlesome and irresponsible queen, Marie Antoinette.

It was a fiscal crisis that precipitated the French Revolution. The cost of war meant that by 1789 half of the tax collected paid the interest on the debt, and the crown was running out of credit. Early attempts at reform failed as these required taxing the nobility and clergy. But in 1788 the situation was so desperate that the king called a meeting of the **Estates General** to consider a tax on all Frenchmen.

When the Estates General met in 1789, things did not work out well for the king. In June, 1789, when the third estate, locked out of its meeting room, met on a tennis court and swore not to disband until France had a constitution. The king yielded, ordering the first and second estates to join the third and vote on measures by head, not estate. Absolutism had come to an end, and the King's power been greatly diminished.

Then on July 14, a Paris mob attacked the Bastille, the fortress and prison that represented royal authority in Paris, and killed its governor. Fearing their masters would turn against them, some peasants in the countryside destroyed the manors of their seigneurs in what became known as the Great Fear. On October 5, 1789, a mob of women, angry over bread prices, marched on Versailles in October and abused the Queen, Marie Antoinette.

> **The cost of war meant that by 1789 half of the tax collected paid the interest on the debt, and the crown was running out of credit.**

The mob took the royal family to Paris as virtual prisoners, never to return to Versailles again. The National Assembly soon followed, setting up the national government in Paris, an indication of the growing importance of the mob. In three months, the **ancien régime** had crumbled, something hardly expected when the Estates were called in May. What had begun as a liberal, fundamental reform of the kingdom fell prey to the violence and intimidation of the Paris mob. The French Revolution had begun. ∎

Important Terms

ancien régime: The union of throne and altar that characterized the absolute monarch of France before 1789.

Estates General: The meeting of all three estates (clergy, nobility, and people) to advise the king in pre-revolutionary France.

Suggested Reading

Chartier, *The Cultural Origins of the French Revolution.*

Lefebvre, *The Coming of the French Revolution.*

1. What was the primary cause of the French Revolution?

2. The nobility and clergy refused to surrender their privileges in the face of a national emergency. Do established elites always sacrifice the best interests of the nation for their own gain?

The French Revolution
Lecture 22

The French Revolution intended the complete disestablishment of the ancien régime. In August 1789, all feudal rights based on birth were abolished and all Frenchmen made equal. That same month, work began on a constitution that would turn the nation into a constitutional monarchy based upon the principles of Enlightenment thought.

In November, the national Assembly addressed the fiscal crisis by confiscating all Church lands, holding them as surety for the issuing of bonds, known as **assignats**. Soon after, it promulgated the Civil Constitution of the Clergy, effectively making bishops and priests into civil servants. Despite Voltaire's anticlericalism and attacks on the Church, these provisions drove many Frenchmen of all classes and political persuasions into opposition to the Revolution, dividing France dangerously.

The work of the National Assembly culminated in the Constitution of 1791, a document informed by the opinions of the Enlightenment that turned France into a constitutional monarchy in which the privileges of the ancien régime were swept away in favor of a bourgeois social structure: Only adult males with property were eligible to vote. One of the most evident principles behind the constitution was the separation of powers so praised by Montesquieu.

Yet despite the claims of equality found in the *Declaration of the Rights of Man*, French citizens were not politically equal under the Constitution of 1791. About half the adult males in France were disenfranchised, as were all women. The Constitution of 1791 was obviously a victory for the enlightened, property holding, anti-clerical bourgeoisie.

The writers of the constitution had made themselves ineligible for election, meaning the new Assembly would be full of men with no experience in government. Radicals stirred fears of armed intervention from abroad and worked the anger of the Paris mob and landless peasants. Expecting an attack from without, the Assembly declared war in 1792 against the Austrians and Prussians, only to be defeated. The Paris mob attacked the Assembly and threatened the king, in effect overthrowing the legitimate government of the capital.

A lucky victory in 1792 that stopped the Austro-Prussian advance seemed to validate the radicals' position. They managed to change the constitution by giving all Frenchmen a vote and intimidated voters into selecting only radical candidates. The new elected Assembly of 1792 declared France a republic and the most radical members, led by **Maximilien Robespierre** (1758–1794), assumed dictatorial authority. The Terror ensued with countless Frenchmen fed to the guillotine until even Robespierre himself was executed in July 1794.

The writers of the constitution had made themselves ineligible for election, meaning the new Assembly would be full of men with no experience in government.

The result was a relaxing of the most vicious elements of the Terror. In 1795, a more moderate constitution was created under which France was largely well and honestly governed until 1799. But, with the collapse in the value of the assignats and the insecurity of war, it fell in 1799 to a military coup by a hero and adventurer from Corsica: Napoleon Bonaparte. ■

Important Term

assignats: The state bonds issued in 1790 by the Revolutionary government secured by the nationalization of the estates of the Church.

Name to Know

Robespierre, Maximilien (1758–1794): A key figure in the French Revolution and architect of the Terror. A disciple of Rousseau and leader of the Jacobins, he became a member of the legislative assembly in 1789. In 1793, Robespierre was elected leader of the Committee of Public Safety, which was instrumental in establishing the Reign of Terror. In July 1794, after a period of violence incited by conflict among rival political factions and marked by mass executions of enemies of the revolution, Robespierre was deposed and guillotined.

Suggested Reading

Doyle, *The Oxford History of the French Revolution.*

Schama, *Citizens.*

Scurr, *Fatal Purity.*

Questions to Consider

1. Was the Terror the natural conclusion to the events of the French Revolution?

2. France sees the Revolution as a defining moment in its history—its anthem is *la Marseilles*; Bastille Day its national holiday; and liberty, fraternity, equality still a national motto. Given the events of the Revolution, is this recognition appropriate in a liberal, democratic but still traditional society?

The Age of Napoleon
Lecture 23

> The only possible response of monarchical Europe to the events of the French Revolution was war. To the conservative leaders of Europe, the war was a crusade in which monarchy, legitimacy of authority, an established church, property rights, and privilege set out to contain not the country of France but the radical ideas of the revolution.

In 1795, **Napoleon Bonaparte** (1769–1821) assumed the role of First Consul of France, essentially acting as a military dictator. His battlefield victories, however, and the largely positive peace that followed in 1802 permitted him to assume greater status, ultimately declaring himself emperor in 1804.

Napoleon was both a brilliant military strategist and a superb administrator. Besides winning battles against the various alliances formed versus France, he reorganized French law, creating the Code Napoléon. Wherever his army was victorious he swept away the old regime and introduced modern, Enlightenment social and religious principles. He restructured the map of Europe and rekindled national sentiment among many of Europe's oppressed peoples.

Napoleon also restructured French society through recognition and education. He created a Legion of Honor, to recognize great contributions to France. He established the new French aristocracy, granting titles and honors through merit in military and civil service. And, Napoleon created the French system of education—the *lycée*—supporting with scholarships boys from all social backgrounds. In 1813, a university system was established, making France one of the most advanced states for higher and technical education.

But other states were very hostile to the French and their reforms. The Spanish hated the French who had put Napoleon's brother, Joseph, on the throne. The Austrians resented Napoleon's victories and the loss of their ancient title of Holy Roman Emperors. And the British both detested and feared Napoleon, as he threatened to invade their island. It was this growing hostility across the continent and his attempt to defeat England through economic isolation that led to Napoleon's fall.

Napoleon's Continental System, designed to close Europe to English trade, was being broken by Russia. He invaded that vast empire in 1812 only to see his huge Grande Armée defeated by winter rather than by arms. Simultaneous insurrections in Spain were aided by the British whose expeditionary force won battles against French troops and found a leader equal to Napoleon: the future Duke of Wellington. Surrounded and defeated, with huge allied armies advancing on France, Napoleon abdicated in 1814 and was exiled to Elba.

When Russian Czar Alexander I refused to support the Continental System, Napoleon invaded Russia with 600,000 soldiers. There was very little military contact but the effect of the starvation and winter resulted in about 575,000 men either dying or deserting, never to be found.

Louis XVIII was placed on the French throne by the allies, and a monarchist terror briefly swept France as those who had suffered under the Revolution now exacted their revenge. Napoleon's quixotic 100 days—his escape from Elba and subsequent defeat at Waterloo in 1815—was only a heroic addendum. The allies who gathered in Vienna to deal with the aftermath of war felt even more strongly the need to contain revolution and deal somewhat more firmly with France. ■

Bonaparte, Napoleon (1769–1821): Brilliant revolutionary general, first consul, and then emperor of the French. Educated at the elite military academy in Paris, he rose to power during the years of the First French Republic by successfully campaigning against the enemies of Revolutionary France. His military campaigns initially defeated every major power on the Continent except Britain. However, his failures in Russia and Spain resulted in a vast coalition against France that defeated Napoleon in 1814. He abdicated the throne and was first exiled with honor, but his attempt to return to France resulted in his second exile, this time to St. Helena, where he died in 1822.

Suggested Reading

Asprey, *The Rise of Napoleon Bonaparte.*

———, *The Reign of Napoleon Bonaparte.*

Questions to Consider

1. Was Napoleon the culmination or the betrayal of the French Revolution?

2. Napoleon's armies spread the principles of the revolution and the Enlightenment, as well as the Code Napoléon, through war. Is it justified to impose progressive ideas and institutions through military conquest?

The Congress of Vienna
Lecture 24

The leading allied powers were all represented at the Congress of Vienna. Three key principles guided the delegates: compensation for the victors, legitimacy through the restoration of deposed monarchs, and maintenance of a balance of power to assure peace.

Despite the conflicting ambitions of the great powers and the complex situation in France, statesmanship triumphed at Vienna, with the collective decision not to crush France or her allies. This would ensure a quick return to European stability and also secure Louis XVIII on his throne, for it was believed that a humiliating peace would undermine Bourbon legitimacy.

Still, France paid an indemnity and was returned to its 1792 borders. Louis was advised to refrain from reconstructing the old regime and to maintain some liberal reforms, including a constitutional charter.

The Congress of Vienna was one of Europe's greatest diplomatic successes, with the great powers willing to compromise to return the continent to peace after so many years of war. The negotiations at Vienna succeeded primarily because they dealt with political realities rather than abstract principles. The Congress was not concerned with freeing

Library of Congress, Prints and Photographs Division.

The House of Bourbon was restored with Louis XVIII, the younger brother of Louis XVI.

various nationalities from foreign control: Italy and parts of central Europe were simply handed back to the Austrians; Poland remained divided.

The ecclesiastical lands in the former Holy Roman Empire were simply amalgamated into secular states, with no concern for the pope's objections. But any remnants of feudalism were also erased, and the Code Napoléon, which had followed Napoleon's armies across Europe, remained where it had been established.

Although a realistic peace was achieved, fundamental divisions persisted. Conservatives, like Austria's **Clemens von Metternich** (1779–1859), remained the most powerful figures until 1848 and used reactionary oppression and the support of the privileged classes and the Church against liberals and the revolutionary fervor that had so unsettled Europe. These conservatives—often from the old nobility—had no interest in freedom of speech or association or inalienable rights.

To ensure that revolutionary ideas would never again arise, the Congress agreed to form the Quadruple Alliance of Russia, Prussia, Austria, and Britain to police Europe, to stop revolution, and to keep Napoleon and his family from power. These reactionary principles, however, could not withstand changes in Europe that were challenging every assumption of established power.

Although the Congress was remarkably successful in restoring peace to Europe, that did not mean that there were not to be tensions in Europe during the next century as there were widespread revolutions in 1830 and again in 1848. Liberalism, nationalism and industrialism would soon prove far greater threats to the established order than the French Revolution or Napoleon had ever been. A more potent Revolution—the Industrial Revolution—was already in the process of changing every aspect of European life. ■

Metternich, Clemens von (1773–1859): Austrian diplomat and statesman, Metternich became a foreign minister of the Austrian Empire in 1809 after Napoleon's capture of Vienna. A major figure in the negotiations before and during the Congress of Vienna, he was called to settle the many issues that arose from the Napoleonic and Revolutionary Wars. His policy, considered a prototype of modern foreign policy management and diplomatic practice, succeeded both in reintegrating France into the fraternity of Europe monarchies and imposing a very conservative regime on most of the continent, particularly in Austria.

Suggested Reading

Kissinger, *The World Restored.*

Zamoyski, *Rites of Peace.*

Questions to Consider

1. Account for the remarkable success of the statesmen who met at Vienna in establishing a state system that would last for almost a century and reduce the incidence of European wars.

2. Prince Talleyrand, the French representative at Vienna, said of the Bourbons in 1815 that they had learned nothing but forgotten nothing. Could the same be said of the statesmen and rulers who fashioned the Congress of Vienna?

The Industrial Revolution
Lecture 25

> The Industrial Revolution had far greater consequences than even the French Revolution. The change from an agricultural or trading society to one based upon the production of goods to be sold was one of the transformative events of European history. The coordination of capital, raw material, labor, and markets required great effort and managerial skill; but the rewards were enormous and benefited both the capitalists who engineered this system and the nations in which they worked.

Capitalism had flourished first in Italy, then in the Low Countries, and expanded throughout Europe in the 16th and 17th centuries. The capitalist system was founded upon the twin pillars of private property and the profit motive. These proved sufficiently powerful to withstand the centralization and restrictions on trade and commerce imposed by **mercantilism**. Capitalism also proved sufficiently flexible and dynamic to meet market demands resulting from the rise of consumer consumption in the late 17th century, to uncover new markets, and to create new demand so as to increase profits.

Adam Smith (1723–1790) was responsible for articulating the ideas of Enlightenment economic theorists that underlay the practice of capitalism. He expounded his ideas in *An Inquiry into the Nature and Causes of the Wealth of Nations* (1776), which has become the bible of laissez-faire capitalism.

The Industrial Revolution occurred first in Britain, and the reasons for this are complex but exemplary. Britain had the necessary concentration of capital, having established in 1694 the Bank of England which ensured ready credit and a stable currency. It enjoyed significant natural resources like coal and iron needed for mechanized factory production. And as an island with a complex river system, Britain could transport heavy materials over long distances to concentrate production. Also significant, English agriculture was extremely efficient, with food production sufficient to feed large numbers of people working in industry. In addition, better nutrition, fewer pandemics, and no major wars fought on English soil helped fuel an explosion in population. This increase provided both cheap labor and ready markets for manufactured goods.

Traditional British freedoms provided the intellectual energy underlying this revolution. Freedom of speech permitted the flow of technical and economic information. Free association permitted the development of trade organizations. Freedom of religion allowed non-conformists to attend their own technical colleges, offering practical and scientific education in no way restricted by social expectation and conservative views. These advantages were reinforced by the inventiveness of the British, particularly the Scots.

Finally, the rule of law gave added support. Parliament put merchants, manufacturers, and entrepreneurs close to government policy and circumvented the injustices of royal monopolies and centralization that encumbered continental enterprise. Equally, the separation of powers and

Adam Smith is considered the father of the modern political economy.

the rule of law made contracts enforceable and officials accountable. So it was that in the century between 1750 and 1850 Britain moved from being a small, prosperous, agricultural island to become the workshop of the world. ∎

Important Term

mercantilism: The centralized regulation of trade and commerce to ensure that no profit would be lost to the nation.

Smith, Adam (1723–1790): Scottish philosopher and economist, considered the father of modern political economy. Smith was among the first thinkers to advocate a free market economy as more productive and more beneficial to society, opposing the prevalent theory of mercantilism and economic protectionism. He also formulated and advocated the importance of the division of labor in industry and manufacture to increase productivity.

Suggested Reading

Ashton, *The Industrial Revolution, 1760–1830.*

More, *Understanding the Industrial Revolution.*

Questions to Consider

1. Why was Britain the first nation in Europe to industrialize; what was its greatest advantage?

2. Does technological and economic change always result in social and political transformation?

The Industrial Working Class
Lecture 26

All of the manifestations of the Industrial Revolution of the 18th century continued into the 19th century, but with much more force. The movement towards industrialization and an industrial society was cumulative. England was almost completely industrialized by the 1860s and 1870s and had become the single largest producer of goods in the world.

From the Industrial Revolution came an entirely new class in European society: the class of those who worked for wages. Significant increases in population created a vast pool of workers. So, too, did the process of rationalized agriculture, which drove many small tenant farmers off the land. More people meant a larger labor pool, so wages did not always rise, and in some cases they actually declined.

The factory system transformed the working environment, with the clock on the wall regulating the work force, robbing it of its former independence. It required individuals to leave their homes and to move to where the work was. The decline of the old, cottage-based textile production system, by constricting the small amounts of discretionary income available to the rural poor, forced rural families to send their wives and daughters into the factories.

But the factories were where power, raw material, or markets were located, not where population had pooled in the centuries of the agricultural economy. Hence, there was a vast population shift in England to the north; in Germany, to the Saar and Ruhr Valleys, Saxony and Silesia; in the Austrian Empire to Bohemia; and in France to the Seine and Rhone Valleys and Lorraine. Rural families left villages where their only support networks existed, making them totally dependent on their employers.

This population migration made huge cities of what had only decades before been small towns. Yet life in the new industrial slums was tenuous, with deaths exceeding births in most cases. Family violence, drunkenness, incest, and prostitution were everywhere in the slums. Also, economic and social change had overtaken political action. There was no social assistance or legislation. The working class included men, women, and children because all had to work to survive. There were no safety controls in factories, with maiming and disease pandemic. There was no sanitation or ventilation. The hours were long and grinding.

It was not just callousness that underlay this early working class exploitation: Social and economic change had simply happened too fast. Those who controlled governments were either well-off urban professionals or landowners who felt pity but also helplessness. There were also moral theories that justified the exploitation of the industrial poor. Again, early industrial concerns were tenuous and highly competitive, so it was feared that high labor costs could cause bankruptcy.

Believing their employers, the state, and the Church cared nothing for their welfare, industrial workers embraced ideologies invented specifically for

© Photos.com/Thinkstock.

The working class included men, women, and children because all had to work to survive.

them and their condition: They flocked to the meetings of the socialists and communists who at least promised some salvation. ■

Suggested Reading

Engels, *The Condition of the Working Class in England*

Thompson, *The Making of the English Working Class*.

Questions to Consider

1. Why were the conditions for the poor in the early Industrial Revolution so terrible?

2. The Industrial Revolution has been called the greatest revolution in European history. Do you agree?

Capitalism and European Society
Lecture 27

Industrialization shaped the world as we now know it, creating new classes, new wealth, new cities, new goods and services, as well as new ideologies. By mid-century governments across Europe began experimenting with labor legislation, and a dynamic new stage of industrial production permitted higher wages and better working conditions.

Also, advances in agriculture, fertilizers, and especially railroads and steamships improved the diets of many Europeans. Food could be imported cheaply from abroad and moved quickly around even large nations by rail. With better diets the population again increased, providing more labor and a larger market for goods.

This further growth of industry and transportation was facilitated by new credit and banking systems that permitted the mobilization of vast amounts of capital, providing a good return and some security even to small investors. At least in Western Europe, the growing ranks of the middle class grew entered into the process of industrialization, initiating the golden age of the middle class.

But this caused tension with the traditional classes, as the new classes created by industrialization—the working class and the managerial middle classes—began to challenge the established order for control. New fortunes were being made and men with huge economic power wanted some degree of social influence. In England, and to a lesser degree France, titles and honors once the monopoly of the old nobility were shared with the captains of industry; and new heroes—engineers, scientists, or inventors—were recognized like victorious generals.

Similar recognition did not attend the working poor, however. Middle and upper class leaders blamed their misery on moral failure rather than on their living and working conditions. Saving souls became more important than helping the poor economically or socially, for doing so would reduce dividends, threaten competitiveness, and merely provide more money for drink and debauchery.

To save the poor, in both a literal and spiritual sense, groups like the Salvation Army were formed to work in the industrial slums. The term "army" is significant, as this was a muscular Christianity, where the goal was to fight to save souls and protect the divinely constituted

To save the poor, in both a literal and spiritual sense, groups like the Salvation Army were formed to work in the industrial slums.

social order. Later, groups like the YMCA and YWCA formed: members of the middle class attempted to get the poor off the streets, but always at the expense of a sermon. Temperance societies were founded, but drink was often the only escape available from the desperate lives of the poor.

Established churches were among the worst offenders, with pastors preaching against sin while not addressing the fundamental roots of the poor's misery. By alienating the poor from the traditional church, one of the most powerful instruments of social cohesion and control was removed from their midst, driving the industrial working classes ever more deeply into the organizations of those who offered immediate, tangible, and even vengeful messages. And these organizations were not spiritual but political, often radical and revolutionary. ■

Suggested Reading

Matthew, *The Nineteenth Century*.

Rapport, *Nineteenth Century Europe*.

1. Why were the middle and upper classes often so callous towards the poor during the 19th century?

2. The established churches of Europe failed the poor by preaching against their perceived vices or against the modern world in general. Why could religious leaders not identify the social and economic causes of their degradation?

The Middle Class
Lecture 28

The middle class was not directly a product of industrialization but certainly prospered from it, becoming increasingly influential in the definition and direction of European society, the economy, and government.

Middle class people worked for pay, often enjoyed superior education, and were ambitious. Advancement based on merit, education, skills, and service was now possible across much of European society, though remnants of the old regime still tried to impede such mobility to maintain their social and political privileges.

In many continental countries this growing class was kept out of government. But as its numbers grew, however, so, too, did the middle class's self awareness. Their numbers, particularly in England and France, gave the members of the middle class a powerful political and economic influence. It was a property owning class, entrepreneurial, interested in the acquisition of capital, and anxious to educate itself.

The middle class was composed of professionals who formed the core of the official bureaucracy and the intelligentsia. It also produced the managers of businesses large and small. They favored reforms that might help them reach their aspirations as a class: the right to vote and to serve in parliamentary bodies. They sought liberty and social harmony, as they saw these things as the keys to progress, and modernization was also part of their world view.

Besides the caste marks of education, ideology, and wealth, the European middle classes externalized their status through a distinctive means of dress, behavior and patterns of consumption. The culture and attitudes of the middle class in Western European society were most visibly defined by the Britain of Queen **Victoria** (r. 1837–1901). Respectability and high moral principle became the model of the British middle class.

This was particularly the case with women, who came to dominate the domestic sphere in the 19th century, raising respectability and domesticity to national ideals. The figure of the "angel of the house," who played the role of loving wife and domestic guardian of morality, came to control the sphere of the home, while more and more men left the home to work in businesses and factories.

This social definition, reflecting the economic power of the greatest empire on earth, was emulated both in Europe and elsewhere, so that Victorian Britain came to represent the principles of middle class morality, consumption, social aspiration, and achievement for others to emulate.

However, in Germany, Italy, and other continental states, the middle class embraced not only a distinct set of cultural markers but also the political ideology of liberalism and nationalism.

Reigning for more than 63 years, Victoria was the longest reigning monarch in Britain.

While many of the nobility still saw themselves as cosmopolitan, the middle classes identified more emotionally with their nation states or ethnic groups. ■

Name to Know

Victoria of England (1819–1901): Reigning for more than 63 years, Victoria was the longest reigning monarch in Britain. Her sovereignty coincided with a time of great economic and cultural progress within the United Kingdom and the great expansion of the British Empire. Her reign saw the establishment of Parliamentary democracy and growing prosperity of the United Kingdom, which, because of improvements in medicine, social legislation, technology, and education, was shared more broadly than ever before.

Suggested Reading

Gay, *Schnitzler's Century: The Making of Middle-Class Culture 1815–1914.*

Loeb, *Consuming Angels: Advertising and Victorian Women.*

Questions to Consider

1. The 19th century has been called the golden age of the middle class. Is this description accurate, and if so, why?

2. The Industrial Revolution created the consumer society in which one's possessions identified an individual or family socially and economically. Has this changed, and was this a positive result of industrial society?

Liberals and Liberalism
Lecture 29

Liberalism became the ideology of the 19th-century middle class. It was an attractive statement of coherent principles founded on the interdependence of personal and collective responsibility between the individual and the state.

L iberalism, as applied to politics, comprised a complex mix of freedoms, most prominent of which were based on **utilitarian** values **Jeremy Bentham** (1748–1832). He believed in government providing the greatest good to the greatest number. Bentham sought tangible ends: He became a proponent of prison and legal reform, including abolition of the death penalty. So Bentham saw an important role for government in creating and delivering programs to relieve the suffering of others

But it was **John Stuart Mill** (1806–1873) who became the most powerful voice of British liberalism in the mid-19th century. Mill's philosophy was a combination of rationalism, romanticism, and intellectual culture that accompanied middle-class values, such as the cultivation of feelings and the improvement of character. Mill's most influential work, *On Liberty* (1859), addressed the idea of freedom, defending the individual's right of self protection, freedom of speech and expression.

Mill also argued for an enlarged franchise, as many liberals believed that giving even those without property access to the vote would make them more responsible and better citizens. In addition they advocated penal reform

© Photos.com/Thinkstock.

Jeremy Bentham, known as the founder of liberalism.

and the universal abolition of slavery. Mill called for the emancipation of women in his most controversial work, *The Subjection of Women* (1869). Mill again referred to the rights of the individual, the "natural freedoms" possessed by all humankind—male or female—against the "despotism of custom" that limited the rights of women to freely participate in society.

Generalizing from the platforms and speeches of English and continental leaders, all 19th-century liberals would hold to these basic principles: civil liberty; economic liberty; personal liberty; social liberty; religious liberty; freedom of trade, speech and association; national and international liberty; domestic liberty (that is, freedom and mutual responsibility between husband and wife and the rights of children); the equality of all citizens under the law; and popular sovereignty and the rule of law enacted by free representative assemblies. These were the dreams of 19th-century liberals.

Liberals did more than theorize: they captured seats in parliaments and national assemblies and formed active, powerful, and often ruling political parties. Liberalism was in essence a middle class movement, dedicated to free trade, extension of the franchise, assault on privilege, and the call for responsible government. In England, the great Reform Bill of 1832 extended the franchise and reduced unrepresentative parliamentary influence. Power was beginning the shift to the prosperous middle classes. ∎

Important Term

utilitarianism: The Enlightenment and liberal doctrine that argued that for something to be good it had to be useful to the greatest number possible.

Names to Know

Bentham, Jeremy (1748–1832): English writer, jurist, and a founder of liberalism. Bentham was the architect of utilitarianism, an ethical theory based on the principle of usefulness in which human actions are only judged valid if efficient in ensuring "the greatest good for the greatest number." He supported the movement to reform Parliament, believing it necessary to extend the right to vote to all citizens. Bentham also supported women in their demands for equal rights and maintained that slavery, physical torture, and penalties for homosexuality were not consonant with human rights.

Mill, John Stuart (1806–1873): English philosopher and political theorist who profoundly influenced the shape of 19th-century British thought and political discourse. He supported the freedom of the individual against the unlimited control of the state, advocated utilitarianism and empiricism in logic and mathematics, as well as social and political theory. He was also a spokesman for humane policies in prisons and in the empire and was a powerful and vocal advocate for the rights of women to enjoy full citizenship and personal freedom.

Suggested Reading

Hadley, *Living Liberalism.*

Mill, *The Basic Writings of John Stuart Mill.*

Questions to Consider

1. Why did Liberalism become the dominant ideology of the middle classes in Europe?

2. Account for the failure of most European Liberals to include the rights of women in their policies.

Liberal Government
Lecture 30

In 1838, the Chartist movement was organized to reform parliament so that it could more fairly represent the population as a whole. The Chartists supported manhood suffrage, a secret ballot, no property qualifications for public office, payment for members of Parliament, equal constituencies, and annual elections. Although the Chartist movement ultimately failed, it gave life to the formation of a Liberal party and illustrated again the need for Parliamentary reform.

Political parties as we know them also began to develop in the mid-19th century, with clear platforms and disciplined organization replacing the vague and shifting coalitions of previous bill-by-bill coalitions. By the second half of the century, for example, British politics began to be dominated by **Benjamin Disraeli** (1804–1881), who, although a Conservative, introduced legislation permitting trade unions and establishing public hygiene in clean cities. Disraeli introduced laws to free Catholics from civil restraints and supported repeal of the **Corn Laws**. He was an architect of the British Empire, and he had the courage to introduce the Reform Act of 1867, initially a liberal measure, to pre-empt civil unrest.

It took time to establish himself among the Tories, but by 1868, Disraeli rose to power and revitalized the Conservatives, appealing to the middle class urban voter (traditional Liberal supporters) to build a new consensus that gave the last years of Victoria's reign its character. He was, as Britain's prime minister in 1868 and again from 1874–1880, a great supporter of monarchy and empire. And, for a Conservative, he ironically

Popular novelist and leading figure of the British Conservative Party, Benjamin Disraeli.

championed Liberal causes, passing the Trade Union Act in 1875 and a Public Health Act that same year to improve urban sanitation.

It was **William Ewart Gladstone** (1809–1898) who personified British liberalism in the 19th century. His government worked to free trade, thus driving down prices for the poor. He abolished taxes on paper and books to encourage literacy and education. Indeed, the first Gladstone ministry (1868–1874) established modern Britain, with subsidized local education and supervised school boards, the secret ballot, and competitive civil service exams.

In France, a similar liberal tide arose, resulting in the 1830 revolution that overthrew the reactionary Charles X in favor of his cousin, Louis Philippe, the "citizen king" who supported constitutionalism and the middle classes. He did not survive the revolutionary fervor of 1848, however. A brief republic emerged only to be captured by Napoleon's nephew, **Louis Napoleon** (1808–1873), first as president and then as emperor Napoleon III in 1852.

Political rival of the Conservative Benjamin Disraeli, William Gladstone became the leader of the Liberal Party in 1867.

Napoleon III was "a liberal on horseback," fostering free trade, rebuilding Paris, and making France a modern industrial country. He progressively freed the press and the franchise. He improved hygiene and transportation and permitted trade unions to strike. By the end of the empire in 1870, ministers were responsible to the Chamber of Deputies and a leader of the opposition was elected premier. If the Franco-Prussian War had not intervened, Napoleon III would have remained the most popular ruler in recent French history. ■

Corn Laws: The tariffs on imported grains in England repealed in 1846.

Disraeli, Benjamin (1804–1881): Popular novelist and leading figure of the British Conservative Party after 1844 and the 42nd Prime-Minister of Britain. He was a favorite Prime Minister of Queen Victoria and skillfully advanced the goals of the British Empire abroad. His domestic policy broadened the appeal of the Conservative Party from its narrow, landed, aristocratic base, making it a real alternative to the Liberals in a time of wider franchise, a policy Disraeli supported.

Gladstone, William Ewart (1809–1898): Four times Prime Minister of Great Britain. As leader of the Liberal Party from 1867, Gladstone was elected Prime Minister, establishing himself as the political rival of the conservative statesman, Benjamin Disraeli. Gladstone is known for his lengthy campaign for home-rule for Ireland, as well as for his contribution to the national elementary school program and reform of the justice system and the civil service.

Louis Napoleon Bonaparte (Napoleon III) of France (1808–1873): Nephew of Napoleon I, president of the French Republic (1848–1852), and the Emperor of the French between 1852 and 1870. Napoleon III gradually restored personal and political freedoms, a process that culminated in the Liberal Constitution of 1870. In 1870 he was maneuvered by Bismarck into declaring war on Prussia, resulting in the devastating defeat at Sedan, where he and 100,000 of his troops were captured.

Biagini, *Liberty, Retrenchment and Reform.*

Kahan, *Liberalism in Nineteenth-Century Europe.*

Lee, *Gladstone and Disraeli.*

1. Why was the Emperor Napoleon III converted to Liberal policies for France?

2. Gladstone, Bright, and Mill argued that government, representative of the people, needed to be active in building a fair society by intervening for the public good. Do you agree?

Science and Progress
Lecture 31

In the 19th century, Europeans had more freedom, more disposable wealth, more opportunities, mobility, and goods than ever thought possible. This reinforced an idea that had become popular during the Enlightenment: the idea of progress. Before then, change was merely an attempt to recover what had been lost. But with the Enlightenment, the concept of a predictable and rational universe was born, leaving human activity to those things under human control, such as the economy, government, and society.

It was believed that science would lead the way by providing the tools for identifying what is good and helping structure how to achieve it. As a result, the collection of data became standard in the mid-19th century. Thinkers like **Auguste Comte** (1798–1857), the inventor of sociology, promulgated the science of society, hoping to define and institutionalize social laws for the well being of all. Amazed at the progress made by humanity, Comte believed that the beginning of the 19th century represented the start of the final age in history, an age of ever greater prosperity, peace, and happiness. It was this view that formed his new philosophy which he called **positivism**.

Advances in the pure sciences of chemistry and medicine provided immediate benefits to all Europeans and also instilled the concept of science as the instrument of well-being and progress. Child mortality declined. And the work of Louis Pasteur (1822–1895) and Robert Koch (1843–1910) led to a great decrease of death

French philosopher, Auguste Comte founded positivism and established sociology as an independent discipline.

Library of Congress, Prints and Photographs Division.

through infection and accounted for a substantial increase in life expectancy. Food was also safer, as Pasteur's procedure for pasteurizing milk improved the diets of Europeans and led to a decrease in tuberculosis.

These benefits were bolstered by a surge in technological inventions in the 1850s. The invention of the sewing machine drove down the cost of ready-made clothing and permitted the lower middle classes to sew almost professionally at home. New mining technology allowed for deeper, yet safer, pits, reducing the cost of coal.

The screw propeller on steamships reduced the costs of transport and hence the cost of imported food: for the first time in European history, famine could be avoided. And the Bessemer process allowed for the smelting of even low grade ore, making iron and steel—the foundation of industrial production and the ever-important railroads—even cheaper. The enormous increase in the networks of European railroads and the establishment of standard gauge tracks resulted in cheap, safe, and fast travel across the continent.

There could be no doubt, then, that this was an age in which scientists and engineers were the new stars and progress the new ideology. National pride was—and remains—cited in the language of industrial production, with GNP the new index of success. Europeans thought increasingly in the language of science, making the later revolutions of Darwin and Marx possible. ■

Important Term

positivism: The theory derived in part from Auguste Comte that only science and verifiable truth should be used to guide philosophical, social, political, or economic action.

Name to Know

Comte, Auguste (1798–1857): French philosopher who founded of positivism and established sociology as an independent discipline. Positivism argues that knowledge should only be accepted as reliable if proven from sense experience. As a remedy to social problems France experienced since the Revolution, Comte proposed that the ideal structure of society was a strict hierarchy in which the wealthy, educated bourgeoisie are at the top and entrusted with the government of the state and the welfare of the working class.

Suggested Reading

Arx, *Progress and Pessimism*.

MacLeod, *Heroes of Invention*.

Pickering, *Auguste Comte*.

Questions to Consider

1. Was the 19th-century belief in progress justified?

2. Industrialization and technological superiority gave just four nations control over more than 50 percent of the world's trade by 1900. Was this fair? And do you see any consequences arising from such an imbalance?

19th-Century Optimism
Lecture 32

Liberalism was having a profound a political influence on social and industrial legislation. By the late 1800s governments recognized that workers must be protected against abuses by employers. Child labor, dangerous working conditions, and inhumane treatment of workers were slowly being legislated out of existence. The spread of fundamental social legislation in Europe blunted the attraction of radicalism and also integrated the workers into the democratic political system.

In 1883, the German Parliament legislated health insurance paid for by joint worker-employer contributions. Accident insurance followed in 1884; and in 1889, an age and invalidity program, funded by government contributions, was instituted to provide pensions and disability insurance for older Germans. The success of this experiment led to the enactment of similar laws across the continent.

Life expectancy, nutrition, wealth, and freedom had all increased, at least in the West. Governments legislated for all citizens and social mobility was rampant. The wealth of Europe expanded hugely: The output of British industries was higher than any other country's at 21 percent of the world's trade, while Germany controlled about 12 percent, the United States 11 percent, and France 8 percent—together accounting for over 50 percent of the world's economy. And empires were being created to provide raw materials and markets.

The race for empire and industrial supremacy gave rise to general optimism, but an optimism tempered with fear and apprehension. Comte's emphasis on data—collecting information on industrial output, productivity, and market share—gave European nations not only hope but also fear, as they compared the advantages of their economic, imperial and strategic rivals. The evidence of superiority or fear of falling behind had the effect of seeing other industrial powers as enemies in a dangerous, zero sum game.

The race for empire and industrial supremacy gave rise to general optimism, but an optimism tempered with fear and apprehension.

Imperialism spawned competition, literally producing a race for colonies—the scramble for Africa, for example—in order to get early or first advantage. This rush for empire resulted in the oppression of indigenous peoples and exploitation of their natural resources. The Berlin Conference of 1884–1885, called by **Otto von Bismarck** (1815–1898), saw the European powers carve up Africa in their own interests, with little or no consultation with the colonized populations.

With the atrocities of the Boer War in 1899, however, the urge to expand or found empires subsided, and European powers began to turn back to Europe, strengthen their continental alliances and improve their military, setting the stage for the Great War of 1914–1918, which exploded the European belief in optimism and progress. ∎

Name to Know

Bismarck, Otto von (1815–1898): Conservative Prussian politician and nobleman, who in 1861 became the minister-president of Germany and in 1867 the first chancellor of the North-German Confederation, overseeing the unification of Germany under Prussia in 1871. Bismarck was a practitioner of realpolitik, the Machiavellian political theory that advocated policies based on current necessity rather than ideological or moral convictions.

Suggested Reading

Davis and Huttenback, *Mammon and the Pursuit of Empire*.

Smith, *Engineering Empires: A Cultural History of Technology in Nineteenth-Century*.

Questions to Consider

1. What were the major causes of the search for empires in the 19th century?

2. The late 19th century saw huge improvements in the quality of life for the industrial poor through trade union activity, political representation, and social legislation. This could only be achieved, however, through transferring wealth from the middle and upper classes through taxation and higher wages. Was this justified?

Nationalism and 1848
Lecture 33

In addition to concepts of science, progress, and liberalism, one of the driving factors of the 19th century that would that ultimately lead to the cataclysm of the Great War was the rise of nationalism. The belief that peoples of similar backgrounds and traditions should rule themselves had taken hold during the French Revolutionary and Napoleonic wars. Wherever Napoleon's armies marched, old, composite states were dismembered and reconfigured along national lines. Liberal ideas became mixed with dreams of national self-determination.

The Congress of Vienna that met in 1814–1815 was a great success in stabilizing post-war Europe, but it shattered these nationalist and liberal dreams. In fact, the Great Powers actively suppressed any movements which called for self-determination or political independence. Nevertheless, revolts broke out across Europe in 1830, sparked by the overthrow of Charles X in France during the July Days. These revolutions were quickly suppressed by domestic or foreign troops.

Nationalism was central to the events in the German-speaking lands of central Europe. The Austrian Empire was a mosaic of nationalities, including Germans, Czechs, Slovaks, Hungarians, Poles, Serbs, Croats, and Italians. The degree of national feeling within each of these groups varied, depending upon the sophistication of their social structures and historical development.

Powerful, supranationalist cultural movements such as **Pan-Slavism**, carefully cultivated by the Russian empire, sought to unite the Slavic (particularly Orthodox Christian) peoples into a family of nations under the protection of the Czar.

In the Austrian Empire, the 1848 revolutions opposed the system established at Vienna and sympathized with nationalist sentiments, although they first broke out in Paris against the "citizen" king, Louis Philippe. In Austria, the revolt's early success almost caused the disintegration of the Habsburg Empire. Liberal students captured Vienna, and **Louis Kossuth** (1805–1894) led a revolution to separate Hungary from Habsburg rule. But the revolution was suppressed in Vienna, and the Hungarians threatened their large Slavic minority, causing a counteroffensive that returned Hungary to the Habsburgs.

The failure of the 1848–1849 revolutions in the Austrian Empire changed the nature of the Habsburg Empire into a more centralized state, united by communications, tariff barriers, and an aggressive policy of Austrianization. The empire was seen by the peasants—regardless of their nationality—as a paternalistic government that protected them against the depredations of their landlords. Thus the Austrian Empire was able to survive the nationalist threats of 1848–1849 until the collapse of the empire after the First World War, which destroyed the ties that bound the nationalities together into an effective union of disparate peoples.

The Austrian Empire was a mosaic of nationalities, including Germans, Czechs, Slovaks, Hungarians, Poles, Serbs, Croats, and Italians.

Similar revolutions broke out in Germany and Italy in 1848. However, even though they, like the revolutions in the Austrian Empire, were repressed, the nationalist movements persisted. This led to a much different outcome in the two great unification movements in the 1860s: the creation of Italy and Germany. ■

Important Term

Pan-Slavism: The 19th- and early 20th-century belief that all Slavic peoples are linked through a common culture, traditions, linguistic base, and orthodox religion, supported by imperial Russia as the only Slavic great power.

Name to Know

Kossuth, Lajos (Louis) (1802–1894): Hungarian politician, jurist, and a leader of the Hungarian Revolution of 1848–1849, serving as Governor-President of Hungary. Having launched a political and military campaign against the rule of the Austrian Habsburgs as kings of Hungary, Kossuth initially succeeded in separating Hungary from the Habsburg crown. Unfortunately, his government's policies alienated those groups who believed they enjoyed greater freedom under the Austrians and an army led by a Croatian noble, Baron Jelacic, invaded Hungary and defeated Kossuth. He continued to agitate for Hungarian independence while in exile, realizing in the admission of Hungary to equal participation with the Austrians in the Austro-Hungarian Empire the 1867.

Suggested Reading

Rapport, *1848: Year of Revolution.*

Sperber, *The European Revolutions, 1848–1851.*

Questions to Consider

1. Is it reasonable that people with the same ethnic origin, language, traditions, and religion should always rule over themselves in a nation state?

2. Was nationalism the most important religion of the 19th century?

The Unifications of Germany and Italy
Lecture 34

The nationalist movements in Europe in the 19th century involved virtually the entire continent. Almost every major nation was to some degree convulsed by the experience of 1848. From that experience arose powerful programs of national self-determination. And two of these— in Germany and Italy—brought about the creation of new states— national states linked by language, culture, and ethnicity.

Napoleon had greatly facilitated the process of German unification by ending the Holy Roman Empire in 1806, turning Austria into the Austrian (and, after 1867, Austro-Hungarian) Empire, increasingly centered around its Danube kingdoms. The Congress of Vienna contributed by suppressing a number of small independent states, resulting in far fewer German-speaking countries. The customs union (**Zollverein**) of the 1830s had brought most German-speaking territories into an economic union that fostered interdependency and closer ties.

In Germany, those national aspirations would be directed and controlled by Otto von Bismarck, the Prussian First Minister from 1862 to 1890. Bismarck set out to unite Germany into a single state that excluded Austria and benefited the most powerful of the German kingdoms, Prussia. Under Bismarck's aggressive policies, the German-speaking peoples of central Europe began to unite under the Prussian crown. Bismarck saw war as his most effective instrument. He was the model practitioner of realpolitik, the very pragmatic policy wherein "the ends justify the means." Prussia fought the Danes in 1864 and in 1866 humiliated the Austrians, unifying all of northern Germany under King William of Prussia.

Bismarck was also able to establish a constitution, with the lower house elected by universal manhood suffrage. This step galvanized the support of liberals and socialists, who now supported Prussia; and in 1870, Prussia united the remainder of Germany by inciting war with France. The Franco-Prussian war (1870–1871) saw Napoleon III's armies defeated and the collapse of his Second Empire. A united German Empire was proclaimed, with Wilhelm of Prussia becoming the Emperor (Kaiser) Wilhelm I at the Palace of Versailles on June 18, 1871. Soon after, the peace treaty with France gave the new empire the French provinces of Alsace-Lorraine, establishing the borders of both nations until the First World War.

Italian nationalist and political figure Giuseppe Garibaldi.

The **Risorgimento** (Resurgence), as Italian Unity was soon known, was accomplished at almost precisely the same time as the unification in Germany. In Italy, various groups desired unity: republicans under **Giuseppe Mazzini** (1805–1872); monarchists under Sardinia's house of Savoy; and Catholics under the pope. It was, though, the House of Savoy, guided by **Camillo di Cavour** (1810–1861), that triumphed. In the 1850s, with the help of the French, the Austrians were driven from northern Italy.

In the south, it was an adventurer, **Giuseppe Garibaldi** (1807–1882), who helped complete Italian unification by defeating the Neapolitan Bourbons in Sicily. A revolt in Naples sealed the fate of the former King of the Two Sicilies, and Garibaldi then ceded the territory to **Victor Emmanuel II** (1820–1878)of Savoy, who was proclaimed King of Italy in 1861. Finally, in 1870 the Italian kingdom captured Rome as its new capital. ■

Important Terms

Risorgimento: The "resurgence" or national unification movement in Italy from the age of Napoleon until the creation of a united Italian monarchy in 1861 and capture of Rome in 1870.

Zollverein: The customs union of German-speaking territories established first by the Prussians in 1818 but expanding until 1866 to include almost all the German states.

Names to Know

Cavour, Camillo di (1810–1861): Italian statesman. As Prime Minister of the Kingdom of Piedmont-Sardinia, Cavour played a central role in the unification of Italy under the authority of the king of Piedmont, Victor Emmanuel II. Following unification in 1861, Cavour was made the Prime Minister of Italy, but he died soon afterwards. In addition to his political activities, he wrote important works on such diverse themes as taxation, agrarian development, economics, and railway construction.

Garibaldi, Giuseppe (1807–1882): Italian nationalist, military adventurer, and political figure. Garibaldi joined the Carbonari, a secret nationalist society whose main goal was to liberate Italy from the Austrians. He participated a series of campaigns, a couple leading him to flee Italy. In 1862, he was wounded by the Italian regular army when he attempted to use volunteers to capture the city and the remaining papal territories, an adventure not supported by the king. Despite this event, Garibaldi continued to fight and work for the complete unification of Italy, fighting the Austrians in 1866 and agitating for the capture of Rome.

Mazzini, Giuseppe (1805–1872): Italian politician, patriot, writer, and philosopher, who played an important role in the struggle for the unification of Italy and in the movement for the liberal reform of politics. In 1831, Mazzini became the founder of the revolutionary movement Young Italy, which aspired to unite Italy and to liberate it from Austrian rule. Mazzini continued to take part in all revolutionary events in Italy during and after 1848, despite living in exile or in hiding.

Victor Emmanuel II of Italy (1820–1878): King of Sardinia, Piedmont, and Savoy, and, after the unification of Italy in 1861, the first king of Italy. He was greatly indebted to the diplomatic and military talents of his Prime Minister Camillo Cavour, who managed the policies of Italian unification for the House of Savoy and convincing the king to maintain liberal, secular policies to unite all Italian nationalists behind his cause. In 1870, the king ordered his army to capture Rome and what remained of the Papal States, initiating a division between the Church and the liberal Italian monarchy that would endure until 1929. Victor Emmanuel became a symbol and a hero of the Risorgimento and contributed significantly to the creation of the modern Italian nation.

Suggested Reading

Beales, *The Risorgimento and the Unification of Italy*.

Farmer and Stiles, *The Unification of Germany 1815–1919*.

Korner, *The Politics of Culture in Liberal Italy*.

Questions to Consider

1. To unify Germany, was Bismarck's policy of realpolitik (the ends justify the means) legitimate?

2. Was pope Pius IX right in refusing to recognize the united Kingdom of Italy with Rome as its capital?

Darwin and Darwinism
Lecture 35

The optimism of the middle classes in 19th-century Europe was based on a belief in science and progress. From the time of the Enlightenment the role of God had been diminished, inasmuch as science had shown that the natural universe operates under immutable laws which do not require monitoring by any deity. Science and technology had established a system of thought and a method for solving problems that had resulted in the huge and obvious economic, social, and political advances of the 19th century.

But the model of God as the great engineer or creator who built the machine persisted. Furthermore, the union of throne and altar formed after the Napoleonic Wars to impose social control reinforced the role of religion, established churches and Christian morality. And the European middle classes embraced these values fervently. Then Darwin's *On the Origin of Species* (1859) burst onto the European firmament with a message that exploded like a bomb: evolution.

Charles Darwin (1809–1882) came from a distinguished intellectual and wealthy middle class family. A superb natural scientist, he travelled much of the world as resident scientist on a British naval ship, the *Beagle*. This permitted him to collect specimens from places where no evidence had been studied before. His conclusions shocked the world and undermined the very foundation of religion and traditional thought.

Darwin proved that species evolve as a consequence of natural selection. He noted that the many offspring of any species are born with small variations and that these minor variations determine which of these offspring will survive to reproduce themselves and these differences. Life, then, becomes determined by random variation: there is no order, no plan, no creator: God is nowhere.

These ideas were not altogether new. But Darwin offered ineluctable scientific evidence as opposed to mere theory. To dismiss him was to dismiss science; to embrace him was to dismiss the foundation of western Christian thought and the established order.

There were still those who argued that the human species developed independently, free of evolution, a privileged, divinely created species with a unique destiny and possessed of unique qualities, such as reason and a soul. Darwin was aware of the controversy that would arise if he placed humans into his theory, so it was not until 1871 that Darwin finally addressed that critical issue in his *Descent of Man*, putting humanity firmly back into nature rather than above or outside it.

Darwin proved that species evolve as a consequence of natural selection.

If Darwin is right, survival alone by any means becomes the purpose of life, the true teleology of humanity. What is good is what works to help a species survive and increase. There is no place in such a system for God or for absolute principles of morality. The line was thus drawn between those who now had to accept the established order and religion purely on faith and those who were compelled to admit to scientific evidence. Europe divided—a division that remains to this day. ■

Name to Know

Darwin, Charles (1809–1882): English naturalist, traveler, and biologist. Darwin was one of the first scientists to demonstrate that all living organisms evolve over time from common ancestors. His theory proved that the principle of evolution depended on natural selection. In 1871, Darwin proposed the same theory for human evolution. While evolution was acknowledged as a demonstrable fact by most scientists after 1859, Darwin's work divided Europe between those more comfortable with traditional explanations for natural phenomena and those keen to embrace science.

Suggested Reading

Aydon, *A Brief Guide to Charles Darwin, His Life and Times*.

Ridley, ed., *The Darwin Reader*.

Questions to Consider

1. Why was Darwin's *Origin of Species* such a revolutionary text?

2. Is it fair to speak of a pre- and post-Darwinian world?

Social Darwinism
Lecture 36

Many aspects of social Darwinism developed from the reading or misreading of *The Origin of Species*, a work that dealt with plants and animals, not humans or societies. Yet Darwin's evidence appeared to reinforce a wider set of ideas pertaining to human social organization, and this has been named, unfortunately for Darwin, Social Darwinism.

Darwin's disciple, **Herbert Spencer** (1820–1903), defined Darwin's natural selection as "survival of the fittest," which, applied to contemporary society, opened a Pandora's box of social, political, and racial attitudes amongst Europeans that severely challenged notions of social conscience. Militarism, war, imperialism, uncontrolled competition in business, apathy and hostility toward the poor and weak, and supremacist racial theories, which obviously pre-dated Darwin, found new life when Darwinism was applied—often mistakenly—to them.

Darwin, for example, was used to justify laissez-faire capitalism. It was argued that the wealthy are successful simply because they have the necessary variations in character—variations like intelligence, diligence, and thrift—while the poor are indigent simply because they lack those positive attributes. Socialism is consequently wrong as it interferes with the competitive instinct that drives progress, and it removes the rewards of success. This argument enjoyed widespread acceptance across Europe, deepening the wedge between the middle and working classes.

At an individual level, Social Darwinism questioned the treatment of the infirm and weak: Should they be permitted to breed and pass along their defective genes? This gave rise to theories of eugenics and challenged the appropriateness of charity. Taking a different approach, others used Darwin to argue that our consciences and complex social structures are the product of our evolution and hence give us the responsibility to provide for the poor and weak.

Again, the competition among nations for raw materials, markets, and dominance led to the application of a Darwinian vocabulary to international tensions. Only the fittest nations would survive, while weaker nations must admit to inferiority and subordination. Characteristics like discipline and physical strength were praised, and entire nations embraced concepts like mandatory military service or the Boy Scouts. War was seen as the laboratory of this theory of superior versus inferior nations and as an instrument of evolution.

Library of Congress, Prints and Photographs Division.

A disciple of Darwin, Herbert Spencer extended Darwin's natural selection into the realm of sociology and ethics.

The natural extension of this was to justify the worst excesses of European imperialism: the appropriation of wealth, dismissal of culture, and slaughter of natives. Because they were able to do this, went the argument, Europeans were by definition superior. This brutal approach was modulated by missionaries who argued they could at least save native souls, and by cultural supremacists who spoke of the white man's burden to disseminate civilization.

What had begun as a theory to explain the evolution of plants and animals had been reinterpreted over the half century after 1859 to support competition among individuals, corporations, nations, and races, predicated on the idea of the survival of the fittest. These attitudes would lead to callousness towards the poor, deadly competition among nations and theories about racial differences which would lead Europe into its darkest moments. ∎

Spencer, Herbert (1820–1903): English philosopher, sociologist, and one of the most energetic Victorian theorists of Social Darwinism. Spencer is known for having extended Darwin's natural selection into the realm of sociology and ethics, and for coining the famous phrase "survival of the fittest." He remained throughout his life an ardent opponent of imperialism and militarism, even though he grew conservative in his social and political views towards the end of his life.

Suggested Reading

Barzun, *Darwin, Marx, Wagner: Critique of a Heritage.*

Hawkins, *Social Darwinism in European and American Thought, 1860–1945.*

Questions to Consider

1. Is it reasonable to apply Darwin's theory of natural selection to human beings?

2. Critics of the Social Darwinists argued that human evolution developed our capacity for self-sacrifice, empathy, and community; hence we can escape the most brutal elements of the jungle. Do you agree with this critique?

Socialism and Utopianism
Lecture 37

Social Darwinism produced two fundamental strains: one that saw the world as a jungle in which individuals had to compete; the other argued that it was the group that constituted the Darwinian entity and that it was the group that would define progress and dominance. It was the latter perspective that reinforced a set of ideas that arose, like Darwinism itself, from the Enlightenment and science. These were socialism and utopianism, both of which posited that the world was not a jungle, but a cooperative in which the values of the community were privileged over those of the individual.

The ideology of socialism, in both its Utopian and Marxist articulations, grew directly from two roots: Enlightenment thought and the conditions of the working classes. The first tradition is best defined by **Jean-Jacques Rousseau** (1712–1778) who argued that the existence of private property in the contemporary world had alienated humankind from its better, purer nature. This principle was applied by those who felt that the work of the French Revolution had been left unfinished. **Francois "Gracchus" Baboeuf** (1760–1797) called for exact imposed equality for all Frenchmen through abolishing private property and forbidding inheritances. **Louis-Auguste Blanqui** (1805–1881), theorizing that owners of property would always side with oppression, went further and advocated changing the established order through concentrated violence and the overthrow of monarchies.

However, it was Count Henri de Saint Simon (1760–1825) who reflected the major current of utopian socialism—one driven by contemporary social conditions. Born a great aristocrat, he yielded his titles and privileges freely and lost his fortune in the economic experiments of the French Revolution. He believed that non-productive classes, especially nobles and priests, returned nothing to society and should be abolished. Rather, an élite of intellectuals should run the nation, control industrial production, and direct the profits towards social goals.

There was the influential **Charles Fourier** (1772–1837), who believed that rational principles of organization could forestall unearned profit and waste. He advocated factory communities (phalansteries) of a mathematically determined 1620 people, all with specific jobs that could be exchanged to prevent boredom. Because universal cooperation and happiness would naturally result, there would be little need for government. Fourier also supported equality among the sexes and gratification of sexual desires, but this had to be done without violence or revolution, which Fourier abhorred.

Charles Fourier, French philosopher who developed models of utopian socialism.

Finally, there was the celebrated **Robert Owen** (1771–1858), a wealthy mill owner driven by conscience to establish a model community at New Lanark. He believed strongly in social engineering and expected that by providing the elements of middle class life, his workers would share the profits of their labor and behave like middle class citizens. Revered by social progressives, hated by

Robert Owen, English social reformer.

other industrialists, he ultimately moved his utopian socialist experiments to America.

None of these thinkers enjoyed personal success—but their ideas and actions continued to be influential long after their deaths. ∎

Names to Know

Baboeuf, Francois "Gracchus" (1760–1797): Known as the Tribune, Baboeuf "Gracchus" (a designation that alludes to the famous Roman reformers, the Gracchi) was a French political journalist and dissenter in the period of the French Revolution. One of the first socialists, Baboeuf was arrested, tried, convicted, and executed for his involvement with the Conspiracy of the Equals.

Blanqui, Louis-Auguste (1805–1881): Blanqui was a socialist activist in post-Revolutionary France. He became the leader of several communist movements, and he edited the radical Swiss journal *La patrie en danger*. Blanqui took part in most revolutionary events in France and spent more than 37 years of his life in prison.

Fourier, Charles (1772–1837): Fourier was a French philosopher who developed models of utopian socialism and proposed the creation of communities housed in four-level apartment complexes where all citizens were accommodated according to a predetermined hierarchy. A graduated income tax would reduce everyone to an essential equality, something Fourier saw as necessary for harmony.

Owen, Robert (1771–1858): Robert Owen was an English social reformer and mill owner who became greatly concerned about the condition of the industrial working class in his factories. He sought ways to improve social, economic, medical, and educational services in company facilities. Hostile to Owen's ideas due to expense and inefficiencies, his partners assured his failure in Scotland. He later tried his experiment in America. When that failed too, he put his energy and his wealth into the trade union movement.

Rousseau, Jean-Jacques (1712–1778): Jean-Jacques Rousseau was one of the most influential thinkers and authors during the 18th-century Enlightenment. Born in Geneva, he fled that city for France, where he was supported by aristocratic female patrons. He wrote *The Social Contract* in 1762, an influential book in which Rousseau fundamentally altered the contract theory of Hobbes and Locke by proposing that men and women in the state of nature were good and that society corrupted our natural virtue. Moreover, when the contract was made to form a society, sovereignty was not surrendered to a king, even one controlled by his subjects, but to the community itself which then became the sovereign General Will.

Suggested Reading

Guarnieri, *The Utopian Alternative: Fourierism in Nineteenth-Century America*.

Sargent, *Robert Owen and His Social Philosophy*.

Questions to Consider

1. What elements were common to all of the Utopian Socialists?

2. The Utopian Socialists wanted to make the problem the solution: that is, to restructure industrial society to distribute its benefits more fairly. Why could this not be achieved through political action, rather than through experimental projects and abstract ideas?

Marx and Marxism
Lecture 38

The working class was increasingly frustrated at the response of legislators and employers to their living and working conditions, so they sought solutions to their problems through socialism. Socialism is a complex and variegated ideology, but its core principle holds that within the capitalist system, the ownership of private property has created economic and social exploitation of humans. It is simply the means of addressing that exploitation that distinguish the various socialist confessions.

Some socialist governments believe that private concerns should be closely regulated in order to achieve social goals. Others wish to end altogether the competitive and exploitive nature of capitalism, a position best represented by Marxism.

Karl Marx (1818–1883) was a German-born theoretician who believed that the study of economics provides the key to understanding the forces of history. He became obsessed with developing a comprehensive scientific system of dialectical materialism that would prove that socialism was inevitable, with all means of production collectively owned by the workers, with no need of capitalists or even, eventually, the state.

The German philosopher G. F. W. Hegel believed that human history was the effort to attain the good. He argued that history was a dialectical process, a progressive idea that was marked by a series of conflicts. Each conflict had two contending elements, the thesis—the established order of life—and

German philosopher, Karl Marx was the major theorist of communism and socialism.

the antithesis—the idea that challenged the old order. Out of this struggle emerged a synthesis, which was not a compromise but a better solution that included aspects of each. This became the source for Marx's later theory of dialectical materialism.

In 1848, Marx composed the *Communist Manifesto* which proclaimed the inevitable overthrow of the bourgeoisie by the proletariat. By 1850, Marx was in London researching *Das Kapital*. The first volume did not appear until 1867, and the next two volumes, edited by his close collaborator, **Friederich Engels** (1820–1895), were not printed until after his death. But *Das Kapital* was the closest Marx came to developing his theory of scientific socialism.

Ironically, Marx was isolated from working class politics, despite the wide adoption of his ideas. The founders of the first Marxist political party in Europe—the German Social Democratic Workers Party—were drawn to his solutions for the working class. But, when this party merged with other socialist groups to bring all German Marxists under a single umbrella, Marx was disenchanted, angered by the inclusion of some non-Marxist parties and in particular by the decision to work for socialist reforms within the German political system.

For Marx saw the very existence of Marxist political parties as self-contradictory: To his mind, the proletariat should never work within the framework of bourgeois politics but be interested only in creating solidarity so as to bring about revolution. Nevertheless, the German party's model was followed throughout Europe. Marxism had superseded Marx. ∎

Names to Know

Engels, Friedrich (1820–1895): Friedrich Engels was a German political theorist and one of the founders of Communism. In 1848 he co-authored with Karl Marx *The Communist Manifesto*. And in 1844, he published *The Condition of the Working Class in England*, which suggested that the only way the working class could improve their desperate conditions was through socialism.

Marx, Karl (1818–1883): A German philosopher, economist, and political journalist, Karl Marx was the major theorist of communism and socialism. In 1848 he and Friedrich Engels jointly composed *The Communist Manifesto*. Although not an activist himself, Marx generated a large and widespread following across the continent. Ultimately, however, much to Marx's disgust, most of these disciples chose to work within the legal framework of political parties or union organizations rather than to foment revolution, a required step for Marx.

Suggested Reading

Marx and Engels, *The Communist Manifesto*.

McLellan, *Young Hegelians and Karl Marx*.

Ryder, *The German Revolution of 1918*.

Questions to Consider

1. Why were Marx's ideas seized so quickly and widely by European socialists?

2. Was the German Social Democratic Party justified in becoming a legitimate political organization, working with the state, while still calling itself Marxist?

Reactions to Rationalism
Lecture 39

The Enlightenment had promoted rationalism: the application of human reason to the problems of society and nature. Newton, Descartes, the *philosophes*, Darwin, and Marx all contributed to the belief that human reason was supreme, operating logically and in an orderly manner to bring progress and wealth.

But in the midst of these rationalists there existed others who were less convinced of the blessings of the 19th century and scientism. Some had witnessed horrible events that contradicted any belief in human reason. Artists sought solace in pessimism, hedonism, aestheticism, or traditional Roman Catholicism, while others joined irrational movements defined by extreme nationalism, anti-Semitism, or authoritarianism. To them bourgeois society was a philistine power that stood between art and all meaningful feeling. And as a result, established society had to be destroyed—a belief that linked the cultural avant-garde with radicals.

The exploration of this irrational side of human nature produced such non-rational schools of thought as symbolism, expressionism, futurism, and Dadaism. Ivan Pavlov (1849–1946) espoused behaviorism, which views human beings as purely psychological organisms whose behavior is a series of physical responses.

On the other hand, his Viennese contemporary, Sigmund Freud (1856–1939), saw human behavior as produced by the unconscious mind (id), which is more powerful than the conscious (ego) and is motivated by very basic urges of power, self preservation, and sex. Society (superego) suppresses those urges so that they are hidden but still operate—and occasionally surface—resulting in aberrant behavior.

Artists looked into the deeper subconscious to produce a different kind of reality, a darker interior vision based on purely subjective understanding. Marcel Proust (1871–1922) sought the real motive for actions "beyond the reach of intellect." Edvard Munch (1863–1944) illustrated the dark night of the soul where reason cannot reach.

Franz Kafka (1883–1924) told a sadder story. The terrible inner world described in his work is one without order, reason, pity, or meaning, a world that is simultaneously absurd and menacing. It was more than fiction, however: it was a prefiguration of life under the totalitarian regimes of Hitler and Stalin.

Friedrich Nietzsche (1844–1900), one of the period's most troubling and misunderstood thinkers, took the irrational elements of the mind—or will, as he called it—and grafted it onto Darwinian theory to create the social theory of supermen who triumphed at the expense of lesser humans. Nietzsche hated democracy, utilitarianism, positivism, the Judeo-Christian religion and the weakness of will that they represented.

For Nietzsche, those religious (and rationalist) virtues—of humility, pacifism, pity, concern for the weak and the poor—should be seen as vices. It was Nietzsche who said in his widely influential work *Thus Spoke Zarathustra* (1883), "God is dead." For Nietzsche, the death of God meant

Friedrich Nietzsche created the social theory of supermen who triumphed at the expense of lesser humans.

there was no longer a single unifying, all powerful, all knowing force in the universe. Instead, we live in a world with no preordained or fixed purpose. These beliefs of Nietzsche would be pernicious and attractive to men who would find homes in extreme groups, such as the Nazi party. ■

Suggested Reading

Gay, ed., *The Freud Reader*.

Hollingdale, *Nietzsche: The Man and his Philosophy*.

Ledger and Luckhurst, eds. *The Fin de Siècle*.

Questions to Consider

1. Why did so many important European intellectuals abandon rationalism in the later 19th century?

2. Can you explain why many of the anti-rationalist avant-garde thinkers of the late 19th century and early 20th century were susceptible to extreme radical political movements?

Fin de Siècle
Lecture 40

Towards the end of the century, Paris had become the cultural and intellectual capital of Europe, so the events of the Franco-Prussian War (1870–1871) had wide influence. The defeat of the French resulted in the abdication of the emperor and the hasty creation of a provisional government which attacked the radical municipal regime in Paris (the Paris Commune). In the ensuing conflict, 25,000 communards were killed and 10,000 transported.

The Third French Republic that emerged in 1875 was inherently unstable, and republican influence began to rise following a series of scandals. A military coup in 1889 was expected, but its leader, General Boulanger, chose suicide instead.

In 1894 the Dreyfus Affair destroyed any popular support for the conservatives, traditional Catholics, and monarchists. A Jewish officer, **Alfred Dreyfus** (1859–1935), accused of selling French military secrets to the Germans, was tried and unjustly convicted. Courageous journalists such as **Émile Zola** (1840–1902) espoused Dreyfus' cause, and France divided into *Dreyfusards* and *Antidreyfusards*. The guilty verdict was overturned in 1906, and republicans assumed control. France was rapidly turned into a secular republic. But there was little sympathy for the growing trade union

Alfred Dreyfus, French military officer whose unjust conviction divided France.

z

Lecture 40: Fin de Siècle

movement. Labor unrest grew until 1910 when a national railroad strike was suppressed.

By 1914, the Third Republic represented only middle class urban, moderate liberal republicans. It had alienated the socialist workers, conservatives, nationalists, monarchists, the army and the church. Tragically, it would be this government that would have to lead the country through its greatest trials: the First World War.

As France experienced upheaval and dislocation, Germany, its greatest enemy, was in a very different position: confident, stable, united, growing in power and influence economically and militarily. In the German Empire, Bismarck created a powerful, efficient state, with a dedicated, paternalistic bureaucracy, impressive social legislation, and exploding industrial base. But the Socialist Party and the Catholic Church remained outside his control.

In 1873 Bismarck began his **Kulturkampf** (culture war) against the church. The Catholics, however, formed a political party, winning many seats in the Reichstag and forcing Bismarck to abandon his policy. In 1878 he moved against the socialists, banning their newspapers and meetings; but workers continued to vote for them and to form youth clubs in support of Marxist ideas.

The Habsburg Empire was extremely conservative with a confused policy towards its increasingly nationalist minorities. The Hungarians attained full partnership in 1867, but the Slavic minorities remained outside. Industrialization occurred rapidly after 1860, creating a working class infected with socialist ideology; but there was little opportunity for reform. Unrest developed both among the oppressed nationalities and among workers and peasants. Affection for the aged emperor **Franz Joseph I** (1830–1916) kept the empire united. But an old monarch was ultimately insufficient to cement together the competing ambitions and policies of this curious, polyglot, central European empire. ∎

Kulturkampf (culture war): The campaign against the Roman Catholic Church in the German Empire waged by Bismarck between approximately 1871 and 1883.

Dreyfus, Alfred (1859–1935): A French artillery officer of Jewish descent, Alfred Dreyfus was accused in 1894 of treason and spying for the Germans. Despite contrary evidence, Dreyfus was convicted, publicly stripped of his army rank, and sentenced to life imprisonment in 1895. Soon a successful campaign was waged demanding Dreyfus's release, accusing the military and right wingers and the press of fabricating the evidence to feed anti-Semitism. In 1899 Dreyfus was officially pardoned, released from prison, and exonerated by a military commission.

Franz-Joseph I of Austria (1830–1916): Franz-Joseph I von Habsburg was the emperor of Austria (after 1867 Austria-Hungary). His 68-year reign was marked by the weakening of the Austrian empire, which suffered ignominious defeat at the hands of the Prussians during the period of German unification. Besides being scarred by political and military failure, Franz-Josef's personal life was tragic with the murder-suicide of his son and his son's mistress and the assassinations of his estranged wife and his nephew (his heir). He died before the disintegration of the huge dynastic empire.

Zola, Émile (1840–1902): Zola was an eminent French writer and journalist of the latter half of the 19th century. His books were powerful social commentaries, particularly *Nana*, about the corruption of elite Parisian society. A courageous defender of Alfred Dreyfus, a republican, and strongly anti-clerical, Zola made many enemies, one of whom perhaps blocked up the chimney in his house, causing his death by carbon monoxide poisoning.

Lecture 40: Fin de Siècle

Suggested Reading

Begley, *Why the Dreyfus Affair Matters*.

Eyck, *Bismarck and the German Empire*.

Schorske, *Fin-De-Siècle Vienna: Politics and Culture*.

Questions to Consider

1. The Dreyfus Affair divided France, and, to a degree, still does. Can you identify another event which polarized any other nation to this degree?

2. France, Germany, and Austria-Hungary approached their problems in completely different ways. Was this because the problems themselves were fundamentally different or because their rulers had varying objectives?

World War I
Lecture 41

The century after the Congress of Vienna in 1815–1815 was one of the most peaceful in European history. However, the conflagration that erupted in August, 1914 was also the most cataclysmic ever endured. The causes were complex, but competition for markets, colonies, and raw materials played their parts, as did the naval race between Britain and Germany. Social Darwinism also provided a rationale—together with nationalism—to create an environment where war was an acceptable solution to international friction.

Above all, 1914 represented a failure of diplomacy and illustrated the dangers of multiple alliances. The **Triple Entente** of Britain, France, and Russia stood opposed to the **Triple Alliance** of Germany, Austria-Hungary, and Italy. No one had anticipated that minor political events in the Balkans would trigger a world war; but when Franz Ferdinand was assassinated by a Serbian nationalist, a series of long-established plans for mobilization and war were activated in the other great powers, making restraint impossible.

When Austria-Hungary declared war on Serbia on July 28, 1914, the Russian Tsar, Nicholas II, mobilized his forces, which set off a chain reaction that none of the crowned heads of Europe, nor their ministers, seemed able to stop. Germany declared war on Russia and France, and then invaded Belgium, bringing Britain into the war. Italy and Japan soon joined the Entente, and the Ottoman Empire came in on the side of the Alliance.

It was universally believed that the war would be short; but stalemate set in on the western front, devouring millions of lives. No one had anticipated the effects of industrialized warfare, of the use of railroads, aircraft, high explosives, submarines, and machine guns that killed and maimed at great distances.

When these could not break the stalemate, poison gas was used, first as cylinders of chlorine and then later fired from shells filled with choking mustard gas. In 1916, the British introduced the tank. But even this technological innovation failed to break the impasse, despite the unimaginable and appalling loss of life, exemplified by two key battles fought during 1916: Verdun and the Somme.

In part, it was their deep industrial bases that permitted Germany, France, and Britain to fight as long as they did; and it was the weakness of those industrial reserves that toppled Russia, in 1917. In that same year the United States entered the war and decisively shifted the balance in favor of the Entente.

By November 1918 an armistice had been signed, but the costs were unimaginable. Combatants had fielded 65 million men of whom 10 million died and 20 million were wounded, victims of the efficient weapons provided by 19th-century industrial society. The map of Europe had changed forever with ancient empires dismembered. There were calls for punishment of the aggressors, Germany in particular. But if a failure of diplomacy and statesmanship had in part caused this "war to end all wars," a similar failure ensured that the peace would not be lasting. ■

Entry of the Americans in World War I gave strength to France, Italy, Russia, and Britain.

Important Terms

Triple Alliance: The alliance among Germany, Austria-Hungary, and Italy at the outbreak of the First World War.

Triple Entente: The alliance among Britain, France, and Russia at the outbreak of the First World War.

Suggested Reading

Meyer, *A World Undone: The Story of the Great War, 1914 to 1918*.

Tuchman, *The Guns of August*.

Questions to Consider

1. Was the First World War inevitable?

2. Propaganda was used extensively for the first time in the First World War. Is truth always the first casualty of any war?

The Treaty of Versailles

Lecture 42

There had been previous attempts at armistice, but all parties had suffered too much to settle for anything short of total victory. The collapse of Germany in the fall of 1918 precipitated the coming of peace.

W hen the United States had entered the war, its president, **Woodrow Wilson** (1856–1924), had defined fourteen points as the basis for any peace to which the U.S. would subscribe. Taken together, these points were an indictment of many of the prevailing ideologies of the 19th century. Woodrow Wilson's Fourteen Points called for an impartial adjustment of all colonial claims, with consideration of the interests of the people involved; declared that the readjustment of frontiers should be effected along clearly recognizable lines of nationality; advocated the autonomous development of the peoples of Austria-Hungary and Turkey; and declared an independent Poland, inhabited by indisputably Polish populations, with access to the sea.

President Woodrow Wilson was welcomed as a hero when he arrived in Paris after World War I.

On November 9, Germany's Kaiser abdicated and a provisional government sought peace based on a modified version of Wilson's Fourteen Points. At 11:00 am on the November 11 the guns fell silent. The treaty was to be negotiated by the leaders of the four major powers: the U.S., led by Wilson, an idealist who knew little of European affairs; France, represented by Clemenceau, a fiery patriot who demanded that Germany be so punished that it could never again threaten France; Britain through its prime minister, Lloyd George, a cynical but astute politician; and Italy in the person of Orlando, who soon withdrew because Wilson refused to recognize the secret treaties that had brought Italy into the war in 1915.

When the German delegation saw the final draft of the Treaty of Versailles, they refused to sign. But the allies threatened to impose it through invasion. Consequently **Friedrich Ebert** (1871–1925), the Socialist leader of the Reichstag, signed under duress. And harsh the treaty was. Germany lost significant territory. It was permitted no air force or submarines, and the army was limited to a volunteer force of 100,000. Article 231 [the War Guilt clause] forced Germany to admit to causing the war and assessed reparations, later set at $33 billion. It was a humiliating defeat.

Friedrich Ebert, leader of the German Social Democratic Party.

Germany's allies suffered as well. Austria, under the Treaty of St. Germain, was forced to recognize the independence of much of the former empire. And, despite Wilson's principles of self-determination, large numbers of Germans were ineffectively incorporated into these new states. Wilson's naive idealism was contained in a plan for a League of Nations that would settle disputes without war, a commitment that Wilson's own United States refused to accept.

As a result, The League of Nations never functioned effectively as an instrument of peace. True, it did much to aid Europe's dispossessed after the war. It collected international statistics, and it served serve as a solid foundation for the creation of the UN after World War II. Nevertheless, it could not stop aggression, nor could it safely protect the world from the rising tide of totalitarianism. ■

Names to Know

Ebert, Friedrich (1871–1925): Leader of the German Social Democratic Party. He was leader of the socialist majority in the Reichstag in 1918 at the end of the First World War. Despite his affiliation with the socialists, he only reluctantly accepted the proclamation of the republic in Germany in 1918 and his election under the Weimar constitution as its first president.

Wilson, Woodrow (1856–1924): U.S. president for two terms, the second of which was marked by U.S. involvement in the First World War. After the war, he traveled to Paris to negotiate the Versailles treaties, for which he was awarded the 1919 Nobel Peace Prize, despite the United States did not join. In 1919, after working hard to build popular support for the League of Nations in the United States, Wilson suffered a stroke which left him partly paralyzed and required his wife to work in his place.

Suggested Reading

Andelman, *A Shattered Peace: Versailles 1919 and the Price We Pay Today*.

MacMillan, *Paris 1919: Six Months That Changed the World*.

Questions to Consider

1. Was the Versailles Treaty too harsh on defeated Germany and her allies?

2. Was Woodrow Wilson justified in refusing to acknowledge the many secret treaties negotiated with Entente allies before the United States entered the war?

The Disintegration of the Established Order
Lecture 43

The collapse of the Imperial German Government and the army came quickly in November 1918, with the announcement that the war was lost, the Kaiser had abdicated, and Germany was suing for peace. The officer corps remained completely loyal to the monarchy and refused to take orders from the socialists leading the provisional government. Meanwhile the empire was disintegrating with separatist movements; the population was starving; thousands of angry, brutalized soldiers were returning home in disorder; and peace had to be made with the victors.

In January 1918, Marxist revolutionaries, **Spartacists**, tried to foment a Bolshevik style revolution. They were opposed by the **Freikorps**, bands of ex-soldiers who had rallied around their officers in the east to oppose communism. When the Spartacists captured Berlin, driving the legislators to Weimar, the Freikorps rallied to dislodge them, crushing cells of communists in Berlin and beyond. The violence was unspeakable, but the Freikorps were identified by most Germans as heroes, having saved Germany from the same fate as Russia.

The Treaty of Versailles paved the way for the new constitution in Germany, a liberal document approved in July 1919 that officially established the Weimar Republic. The new constitution provided for a strong central government and a powerful president, but left local administration in the hands of the various German states. Elections were held, but there was little support for a liberal republic: most influential Germans, nostalgic for the empire, blamed the socialists for their humiliation.

When an attempt was made in 1920 to disband the Freikorps, they marched on Berlin and named a right-wing politician head of government. This right-wing coup galvanized the Spartacists who raised a communist army in renewed civil war. The Freikorps and the regular army had no compunction about suppressing the Spartacists, indicating the weakness of the elected government, the rightist sympathies of the army, and the danger from the left.

The Treaty of Versailles also caused economic collapse. To meet the Allied reparation demands, the Weimar government simply printed more money. The exchange rate soared from 8.9 marks to the US dollar in 1919 to 25 billion marks to the dollar in 1923. The losers were the middle classes and businesses, robbing the republic of its natural support. A rash of political assassinations only added to the disintegration of the fabled discipline of German society. All of which explains the attraction of Adolf Hitler.

To meet the Allied reparation demands, the Weimar government simply printed more money.

At that time, Hitler was leader of a small, radical right wing party in Bavaria with a Freikorps of its own: the SA, or *Sturm Abteilung* ("Storm Section" in English). In an attempt to foment a general right-wing coup, Hitler led his group in 1923 to overthrow the Bavarian state in his Munich Beer Hall Putsch. The coup failed and Hitler was sent to prison for a short period, an opportunity he used to write his own manifesto—*Mein Kampf* (*My Struggle*)—and plan his future, a future which would see Europe descend into a hell even more unspeakable than the slaughter of the trenches of World War I. ■

Important Terms

Freikorps: Bands of paramilitary nationalist veterans, unemployed and bitter over Germany's defeat in the First World War, who fought socialist and communist revolutionaries. Hitler recruited his earliest storm troopers from these groups.

Spartacists: Communist revolutionary bands, inspired by the Bolshevik revolution in Russia, who attempted to foment a similar uprising in Germany after the First World War. The name is taken from Spartacus, the leader of the slave revolt against the Romans in 73 B.C.

Suggested Reading

Kolb, *The Weimar Republic*.

Weitz, *Weimar Germany: Promise and Tragedy*.

Questions to Consider

1. Explain how the mighty Imperial German state could disintegrate so quickly and completely.

2. Can we make comparisons between the collapse of Germany into anarchy in 1918–1919 and the period immediately following the collapse of the Roman Empire?

The Bolshevik Revolution
Lecture 44

Russia was the country least influenced by the ideas that had animated Europe in the 19th century. Russia during the late 19th and early 20th centuries was a backward state inhabiting a vast landmass extending from its eastern border with Prussia (now Poland) to the Pacific Ocean. It was an inharmonious union of a several disparate nationalities under the autocratic rule of the Czar.

The vast majority of Russians were agricultural laborers, an illiterate, conservative, and deeply religious, mass of humanity that was feared by landlords but lacked any politicization. The serfs were not freed until 1861, and there was no constitution or representative assembly until 1905. A telescoped industrialization, including rapid growth in urban centers, railroads, and foreign investment, initiated many of the problems faced much earlier in Western Europe and fomented unrest. The humiliating defeat in the Russo-Japanese War of 1904–1905 reflected the incompetence and weakness of Russia's military.

When Russia entered the First World War, then, it did so without the complex and deep industrial and economic base enjoyed by the other great powers. Its only strength was in numbers—badly trained and equipped soldiers who died by the millions on the eastern front.

The consequent revolt in February 1917 precipitated the abdication of Czar **Nicholas II** (1868–1918) and the establishment of a liberal constitutional government. But, Marxist revolutionaries (Bolsheviks) had been spreading propaganda among the soldiers at the front and workers in the cities to overthrow the provisional government. In October 1918 the Bolsheviks assumed power under **Vladimir Lenin** (1870–1924). He ended the war immediately with the humiliating Treaty of Brest-Litovsk (1918), yielding to the harsh demands of the Germans and Austrians; but he bought peace so that he could build a communist state.

Soon all opposition was removed from government and a secret police established. Not all Russians sympathized with Lenin, precipitating a civil war (1918–1920) that cost many million more lives. After the end of World War I, many European nations sent expeditionary forces to fight against the Red Army, just as Russian communist agents worked to stir up communist revolutions in Germany, Hungary, and elsewhere.

> **When Russia entered the First World War, then, it did so without the complex and deep industrial and economic base enjoyed by the other great powers.**

But Lenin's comrade, Leon Trotsky, was a brilliant organizer. By 1920 his Red Army had defeated all of the anti-communist forces, leaving Lenin free to establish a totalitarian state. To reconstruct Russia's industrial economy, the Party encouraged heavy industry to overcome Russia's backwardness, requiring great sacrifices by the Russian people, whose needs in accommodation and consumer goods suffered. Under Lenin, the Communist Party controlled every aspect of Soviet life. Freedom of speech, religion, association, movement, and thought were brutally suppressed.

Joseph Stalin (1879–1953), Lenin's successor, was even more brutal, killing millions through the forced collectivization of land, purges, and terror. Stalin cared little for the loss of life, talent and experience: through terror he proved his ruthless omnipotence and created a totalitarian state that could only be matched in its iniquity with Nazi Germany. ■

Names to Know

Lenin, Vladimir (1870–1924): Vladimir Ilyich Lenin dedicated his life to Marxist revolutionary activity, both in Russia and during his exile. Smuggled back into Russia by the Germans, Lenin overthrew the liberal democrats and, with the subsequent "October Revolution," Lenin became the first leader of the "State of the Soviets." Soon after the Revolution, Lenin authorized the "Red Terror," resulting in the imprisonment of his opponents and the mass execution of wealthy farmers. Having survived two assassination attempts, Lenin suffered a stroke in 1922 and retired.

Nicholas II of Russia (1868–1918): Nicholas II Romanov was the last Russian czar before the Bolshevik Revolution of 1917 which overthrew the monarchy. He presided over the humiliating defeat of Russia during the Russo-Japanese war of 1905 and the subsequent slaughter of peaceful petitioners in front of his palace that same year. Russia suffered terribly during the First World War, and under this stress the state collapsed. Nicholas and his family were imprisoned during the subsequent Bolshevik Revolution and were murdered under the order of Lenin in 1918.

Stalin, Joseph (1878–1953): Joseph Stalin succeeded Lenin to head the Soviet Union between 1924 and 1953. Stalin eliminated Lenin's policy of limited free trade and private property and replaced it with a system in which the government decided such matters. During the 1930s, Stalin launched the Great Purge, resulting in hundreds of thousands of executions. Stalin cemented his power after the war by imposing communist rule over most of Eastern Europe, forming the Soviet Bloc and initiating the Cold War.

Suggested Reading

Kenez, *A History of the Soviet Union from the Beginning to the End.*

Pipes, *A Concise History of the Russian Revolution.*

Questions to Consider

1. Why did the first Marxist revolution occur in Russia, a backward, largely agricultural state?

2. Given the terror and horror of the Bolshevik state and Stalin's totalitarianism, why did revolutionary Marxism remain such a powerful force in Europe?

Fascism in Italy
Lecture 45

Italy is a curious place for Fascism to have developed: there was no terrible national humiliation, although one was perceived; there had been no collapse of civil or military authority, although the state did become paralyzed; there was no real threat from the extreme left but, again, one was feared.

Despite unification, Italy had remained a weak and hesitant nation fraught with social, regional, and class antagonisms. Italy had few material resources, very little industry, and its agriculture was exhausted by millennia of poor cultivation techniques. Parliamentary government was a sham with its severely restricted franchise. Nevertheless, Italy underwent a remarkable expansion of nationalism after unification, stimulated by nationalist newspapers, journals and politicians.

Stirred by the rhetoric of the Risorgimento, **Enrico Corradini** (1865–1931) founded in1903 a nationalist journal that argued for a new breed of Italian. He declared bourgeois, liberal society too cautious and unheroic for Italy; socialism too cooperative and internationalist. When the franchise was expanded in 1912, his Italian Nationalist Party won three seats. But it was the First World War that galvanized the fascist right and discredited the left.

Italy had been expected to join Austria-Hungary and Germany against the Entente in 1914, but did not. Anti-Austrian feelings remained powerful, and the Entente made rich promises of territory. So, in 1915 Italy joined on the side of Britain, France, and Russia. The fighting was hard, but the peace was worse. At Versailles, Wilson refused to honor the treaties that had brought Italy into the war. Italians felt betrayed. Their economy was in ruins. Socialists and Marxists were stirring up workers and peasants to strikes and violence. As in Germany, angry nationalist ex-soldiers formed bands, identified by their black shirts, to attack socialists and communists.

In this anarchic situation there arose **Benito Mussolini** (1883–1945). Mussolini had been a radical socialist, editor of the party newspaper,

Avanti, but had been converted by the war to nationalism. In 1919 he organized his own band of black shirts using the symbol of authority in ancient Rome (*fasces*) for its emblem. This group became a model for the other black-shirts who broke up communist meetings and protected businesses against strikes and occupation.

Mussolini formed the Fascist Party in 1921 to cement his growing national influence. Sensing victory, he marched on Rome in 1922. When the King invited him to become prime minister, Mussolini quickly used the office to establish a dictatorship. This fascist victory in

Benito Mussolini, an Italian journalist, agitator, and politician who became the leader of the Italian Fascist Party.

Italy became a model for Franco in Spain and Hitler in Germany: it also attracted millions of sympathizers across the continent who feared fascists less than the soviet communists.

By 1925, the Italian state became a one-party totalitarian dictatorship. There was total fascist control of the army, local, and national governments, and the creation of a secret police. Just 65 years after the unification of the kingdom, Italian democracy was dead. ∎

Names to Know

Corradini, Enrico (1865–1931): Corradini was an Italian poet and novelist and founder of the radical right-wing newspaper *Il Regno*, an antecedent to fascism. He was also a founder of the Italian Nationalist Party in 1910. Corradini argued that nations are defined socially, just as classes are; and his strident nationalism encouraged Italian imperialism and militarism. After World War I, the Italian Nationalist Party led by Corradini merged with Mussolini's Italian fascist party.

Mussolini, Benito (1883–1945): Benito Mussolini was an Italian journalist, agitator, and politician who became the leader of the Italian Fascist Party and first, prime minister, then dictator, of Italy from 1922 to 1943. Soon after Mussolini's march on Rome in 1922, the Italian liberal democracy was dismantled, resulting in a one-party dictatorship under Mussolini. Following the Allied invasion of Italy in 1943, Mussolini was deposed and imprisoned. Freed by German soldiers, he established a fascist government in the north of Italy, but was later captured and executed.

Suggested Reading

Bosworth, *Mussolini's Italy*.

De Grand, *Italian Fascism: Its Origins and Development*.

Questions to Consider

1. Why did Fascism develop first in Italy?

2. It is suggested that Italy was finally unified by Mussolini through his centralization of government, propaganda, communications networks, and accommodation with the Roman Church. Do you agree?

The Nazi Regime in Germany
Lecture 46

The instability of the Weimar Republic generated fringe parties spreading angry messages and espousing violent platforms. The National Socialists German Workers' Party (Nazi) was one of these, but when Adolf Hitler assumed its leadership he turned it into both a potent political force and an armed band with its own storm trooper thugs. A failed coup in Munich in 1923 saw Hitler jailed, a time he used to write *Mein Kampf*, his program of racial hatred and Nazi purpose.

Hitler realized that the route to power was not through armed revolution and insurrection but through election. The Nazis were led by Hitler through three progressively successful elections to emerge as the largest party, although still short a majority of seats. The inability of the left to cooperate resulted in a stalemate. So in 1933, Hitler was appointed chancellor. The next month a fire, blamed on communists, damaged the Reichstag; and Hitler demanded that the president decree an emergency, permitting the Nazis to jail opponents and silence their campaigns through intimidation.

In the 1933 elections the Nazis consequently won control of the government. Hitler quickly destroyed the Weimar constitution, turning Germany into a Nazi dictatorship. By 1935 the anti-Jewish platform of the Nazis became law, concentration camps were established, and the secret police (Gestapo) terrorized the minority of dissenting Germans.

National Archives and Records Administration.

Adolf Hitler joined the Nazi party in 1919 and rose rapidly. By 1923 he was its leader.

145

This totalitarian state outlawed all political parties except the Nazis, silencing all opponents. The Nazi symbol, the swastika, replaced the German flag. Total censorship of the press ensued. The Nazi Party took over control of education. The economy and industry were also made subject to the party. As a consequence, Hitler controlled every aspect of German life.

Jews were initially fired from the government and from teaching in schools or universities, while Anti-Semitism and Nazi racial theory became part of the school curriculum. Soon after, they were deprived of their citizenship and their civil rights through the so-called Nuremberg Laws, promulgated in 1935. This anti-Semitic program drove many to Jews to leave Germany, while those who remained were subjected to constant attacks by Nazi thugs. On November 9–10, 1938, Jewish shops and synagogues were attacked during *Kristallnacht*, the night of broken glass.

Hitler repudiated the Treaty of Versailles by reoccupying the Rhineland, rebuilding German armaments, and demanding all Germans be included in his Reich. The weak response of the allies emboldened Hitler. In 1938, Germany and Austria united; that same year Czechoslovakia was required by her allies to yield the Sudetenland; soon after, the rest of the republic was occupied. In 1939, a non-aggression treaty with the Soviets gave Hitler the ability to invade Poland, igniting the Second World War. With binding treaties between the western democracies and Poland in place, Britain and France declared war on Germany on September 3, 1939. The peace after the war to end all wars had lasted only 20 years. ∎

Suggested Reading

Bendersky, *A Concise History of Nazi Germany*.

Evans, *The Third Reich in Power*.

Kershaw, *Hitler: A Biography*.

1. What was the appeal of Hitler and the Nazis to Germans in the 1930s?

2. What were the differences between the totalitarian structures of Nazism and Soviet Communism?

Europe between the Wars
Lecture 47

World War I was not a war to end all wars, nor was it a war to make the world safe for democracy. On the contrary, it destroyed the European state system and economies, incited radical nationalism, and polarized the continent between the extreme right and left, setting the stage for resumption of hostilities in 1939.

Although most major states emerged from the war as functioning democracies, by 1939 only Britain, France, Belgium, and the Netherlands enjoyed true democratic government. The new states created from the old empires were particularly weak. Markets had been cut off from raw materials, and transportation lines disrupted. Nationalism had been further stimulated, but there was often no established state bureaucracy on which to build. Hungary experienced a communist coup in 1919 that created the Hungarian Soviet Republic, but the communists were suppressed by foreign intervention resulting in a right wing nationalist dictatorship.

Equally important in the collapse of democracies across Europe were the appalling economic conditions. There was chronic unemployment, economic dislocation, and the labor unrest. The reparations to be paid by the Germans caused hyperinflation, exacerbated by the printing of money in large amounts by new states that had to build a state apparatus from nothing. There was also the cost of rebuilding the shattered countries of France and Belgium. The result was inflation that made European currencies unstable. Money literally became worthless and the state broke down as a result.

In Yugoslavia the king decreed a royal dictatorship to control nationalist hatreds. The fascist Iron Guard arose in Romania and King Carol imposed a royal dictatorship but abdicated in 1940: the fascists returned in a Nazi puppet state. Nationalism divided Bulgaria, and fascism emerged, driving King Boris to also decree a royal dictatorship, with close ties to the Axis powers. Poland, threatened by Russia and Germany, fell to a military leader, Marshal Pilsudski. Spain witnessed a fascist victory under Franco in 1936.

The victorious democracies also suffered. Britain was crippled by war debt, the loss of markets, and vast unemployment. In 1926, a general strike generated support for the socialist Labor Party, which won the 1929 elections, institutionalizing the ideological chasm between left and right. France was equally burdened by war debt and the huge cost of rebuilding the ravaged nation. The economic chaos of the 1930s further polarized French society: fascist parties grew in popularity; but, unlike in Italy and Germany, the French left cooperated, creating a National Front government of socialists and communists in 1936 that neutralized the threat of a communist revolution while simultaneously reducing the power of the extreme right.

> **Europe between the wars, then, was hardly a celebration of democracy, and the sacrifices of the First World War seemed to have been in vain.**

Europe between the wars, then, was hardly a celebration of democracy, and the sacrifices of the First World War seemed to have been in vain, leading to the observation that the Second World War that broke out in September 1939 represented not a new war but a continuation of the previous conflict, separated by a fragile 20-year truce. ■

Suggested Reading

Kitchen, *Europe Between the Wars*.

Lee, *European Dictatorships 1918–1945*.

Questions to Consider

1. Why did democracy so often fail in Europe between the wars?

2. Was the Second World War really a continuation of the First World War with a 20-year intervening truce?

The New Europe
Lecture 48

This journey through European civilization has traced the paths of a great many of the ideas, events, and individuals who helped define what it was—and is—to be European and, to a degree, Western. Ideas and institutions that were developed in Europe in the context of European conditions and circumstances often found rich lives elsewhere, spread by colonization and by adoption to guide current national practice or form the discourse of dissent.

Concepts such as inalienable human rights, science and progress, industrialism, democracy and rule of law all arose because of events in Europe; and, although these ideas are often challenged and were often crushed, their power persists to define the vocabulary of international relations and national debate. There is no doubt but that Europe today is much freer, more open, and more humane than at almost any time in its troubled history.

Many issues are not yet settled, such as the disjunction between faith and reason and the balance between individual and group rights. Pernicious emotions such as extreme nationalism continue to threaten the peace, not only of Europe but of the world. Powerful ideologies that Europe has largely now rejected, such as communism, continue to thrive in areas to which they were exported, while others, such as fascism, have largely been relegated to the dustbin of history.

Racism continues to operate not only in Europe but everywhere. The principles of racial superiority or privilege are hard to suppress, and although great strides have been made in ending such prejudice, conflict and instability tend to reinforce such ideas even now.

The great wars and other events of the 20th century have largely exploded the belief in progress as an article of faith. Things have improved in many ways: medical care, knowledge of the universe, and our sense of responsibility for the planet. But this does not convince us that progress is inevitable: we are more unsure and tentative than our European ancestors, because we have seen that civilization can be reversed as well as advanced.

No reasonable person could explain the carnage of the trenches, the Holocaust, or the atrocities of the Gulag as anything but a denial of progress and civilization and a rejection of the good principles that gave Europe its dignity. Through such horrors we have lost some of our self-confidence. On the other hand, we gained maturity and perspective, particularly in the knowledge that we cannot allow anything remotely similar to occur again.

Europe is often called the Violent Continent, and much of what has been discussed here reinforces that description. It was indeed a crucible of fire; but from this shared experience has arisen a new idea of Europe. The European Union now embraces much of the continent in a broad economic

The European Union is now a federated union of 27 sovereign states that embraces much of the continent in an economic and loose political association. This dream was achieved through the positive power of democracy, human rights, and liberal legislation, rather than through religion, war, or ideology.

and political association, a dream achieved through the positive power of democracy, human rights and liberal legislation, rather than through religion, war, and ideology. ■

Suggested Reading

Leonard, *Why Europe Will Run the 21ˢᵗ Century*.

McCormick, *Understanding the European Union: A Concise Introduction*.

Questions to Consider

1. Why was there such a strong impetus to establish the European Union?

2. What do you think the future of Europe will be?

Timeline

800..Coronation of Charlemagne
as Holy Roman Emperor.

1054..Separation of Latin from
Orthodox Christianity.

1095–1099.......................................First Crusade.

1215..Magna Carta.

1258–1324......................................Osman, founder of Ottoman Empire.

1293..Florentine Ordinances of Justice.

1304–1374......................................Life of Petrarch.

1305–1378......................................Babylonian captivity of papacy.

1331–1406......................................Life of Coluccio Salutati.

1337–1453......................................Hundred Years War.

1343..Collapse of the Bardi and Peruzzi banks.

1347–1351......................................Black Death.

1378–1417......................................Great Schism of the papacy.

1394–1460......................................Life of Prince Henry the Navigator.

1408–1415......................................Jon Hus preaches in Bohemia.

1409..Council of Pisa.

1414–1418....................................... Council of Constance.

1420–1434....................................... Hussite Revolt.

1389–1464....................................... Life of Cosimo de'Medici.

1449–1492....................................... Life of Lorenzo de'Medici.

c. 1450... Printing with movable type.

1453... Conquest of Constantinople
by the Turks.

1466–1536....................................... Life of Erasmus of Rotterdam.

1469... Marriage of Ferdinand of Aragon
and Isabella of Castile.

1478–1535....................................... Life of Thomas More.

1483... Spanish Inquisition.

1492... Columbus discovers the
Americas; defeat of the Moors of
Granada; expulsion of Muslims
and Jews from Spain.

1496–1498....................................... Voyages of John Cabot.

1498... Vasco da Gama circumnavigates Africa.

1500... Birth of Charles V; Cabral
claims Brazil for Portugal.

1509... *In Praise of Folly* by
Desiderius Erasmus.

1562–1589 .... Wars of Religion in France.

1568 .... Revolt of the Netherlands.

1571 .... Battle of Lepanto.

1572 .... St. Bartholomew's Day massacre.

1589 .... Henry of Navarre becomes
Henri IV of France.

1598 .... Edict of Nantes.

1603–1625 .... James I Stuart on the English throne.

1618–1648 .... Thirty Years' War (Bohemian,
Danish, Swedish, and French).

1620 .... *Novum Organum* by Francis Bacon.

1629 .... Edict of Restitution.

1632 .... Death of Gustavus Adolphus at
Lutzen; *Dialogue of the Two Great
World Systems* by Galileo.

1634 .... Murder of Wallenstein.

1637 .... *Discourse on Method* by Descartes.

1642–1649 .... English Civil War.

1643 .... Death of Richelieu and Louis
XIII; accession of Louis XIV.

1648 .... Peace of Westphalia ends
Thirty Years' War.

1649.. Execution of Charles I; beginning of the
interregnum under Oliver Cromwell.

1651.. *Leviathan* by Thomas Hobbes.

1653–1658...................................... Protectorate in England.

1660.. Restoration of English
monarchy under Charles II.

1661.. Death of Mazarin and beginning
of personal rule of Louis XIV.

1683.. Death of Colbert.

1685.. Revocation of the Edict of Nantes.

1687.. *Principia* (Universal Laws)
by Sir Isaac Newton.

1688.. Glorious Revolution: James II is
replaced by William and Mary.

1690.. *Second Treatise of Government*
and *An Essay Concerning Human
Understanding* by John Locke.

1694.. Foundation of the Bank of England.

1694–1778...................................... Life of Voltaire.

1748.. *De l'esprit des lois* by Montesquieu.

1751–1772...................................... *Encyclopédie* by Diderot.

1759.. *Candide* by Voltaire.

1762 .... *Social Contract* and *Emile* by Jean Jacques Rousseau.

1764 .... Hargreaves's spinning jenny.

1774 .... Louis XVI becomes King of France.

1776 .... *Wealth of Nations* by Adam Smith.

1784 .... Watt's steam engine.

1789 .... The French Revolution begins.

1790 .... Civil Constitution of the Clergy in France.

1791 .... Declaration of the Rights of Man and the Citizen in France; Declaration of Pillnitz (Austria and Prussia against France).

1792 .... The Terror.

1793 .... Execution of Louis XVI and Marie-Antoinette.

1794 .... Execution of Robespierre.

1795 .... The Directory.

1797 .... Execution of "Gracchus" Baboeuf.

1798 .... *Principles of Population* by Thomas Malthus.

1799 .... Napoleon's *coup d'état*.

1802.. Napoleon named first consul for life.

1804.. Napoleon crowned Emperor
of the French.

1812.. Napoleon's Russian Campaign.

1814.. Napoleon abdicates at Fontainebleau;
the Congress of Vienna reinstates
conservatism in Europe; *The
Reorganization of European Society*
by Count Henri de Saint-Simon.

1815.. The Hundred Days (Napoleon's
return from Elba).

1830.. Revolution in France overthrows
Charles X Bourbon; Louis-
Philippe installed as king.

1832.. Great Reform Bill in England.

1837–1901...................................... Victorian Age.

1846.. Repeal of the Corn Laws.

1848.. Revolutions sweep Europe; Louis
Napoleon Bonaparte (Napoleon
III) becomes President of France;
the Frankfurt Assembly; *The
Communist Manifesto* by Karl
Marx and Friedrich Engels.

1857.. Death of Auguste Comte.

1859...*Household Management* by
Harriet Beeton; *Origin of the*
Species by Charles Darwin; *On*
Liberty by John Stuart Mill;
Self Help by Samuel Smiles.

1859–1870.....................................Italian unification.

1860...Garibaldi captures the Kingdom
of the Two Sicilies.

1861...United Italian Kingdom declared
under Victor Emmanuel II.

1864...Syllabus of Errors.

1867...Austro-Hungarian Empire formed;
Second Reform Bill (England).

1867–1883.....................................*Das Kapital* by Karl Marx
and Friedrich Engels.

1868–1874.....................................Gladstone serves as Prime
Minister of England.

1870...Pope Pius IX declares himself infallible;
Italian army captures Rome from the
pope; abdication of Napoleon III.

1871...German Empire declared;
Paris Commune; *Descent of*
Man by Charles Darwin.

1873...Bismarck begins attack on the Roman
Catholic Church in Germany.

1874–1880 .... Disraeli serves as Prime
Minister of England.

1878 .... Bismarck's attack on the German
Social Democratic Party.

1879–1881 .... Franco-Prussian War.

1883 .... Bismarck legislates national
health insurance in Germany.

1884–1885 .... Berlin Conference.

1889 .... Old age insurance introduced
in Germany.

1894 .... Conviction of Alfred Dreyfus.

1898 .... "J'Accuse" published by Emile Zola.

1899 .... *Theory of the Leisure Class*
by Thorstein Veblen.

1904 .... Russo-Japanese War.

1905 .... Revolution of 1905 and
Bloody Sunday in Russia.

1914 .... Assassination of Francis Ferdinand
leads to World War I.

1914–1918 .... World War I.

1915 .... Italy enters the war on the
side of the Entente.

1917.. Revolution of 1917 brings communism to Russia; the United States enters the war on the side of the Entente.

1918.. Defeat of Germany and abdication of William II; defeat of Austria-Hungary and collapse of the Hapsburg empire; Treaty of Brest-Litovsk takes Russia out of World War I.

1919.. Treaty of Versailles; Weimar Republic; Hungarian Soviet Republic under Bela Kun.

1922.. Formation of the USSR; Mussolini's March on Rome establishes fascism in Italy.

1924.. Joseph Stalin assumes power in Soviet Union.

1928.. Stalin's purges and five-year plans.

1929.. Great Depression begins; Lateran Treaty between Italy and the Roman Catholic Church.

1933.. Nazi Party comes to power in Germany.

1936.. Spanish Civil War; German reoccupation of the Rhineland.

1938.. German annexation of Austria; Munich Conference; Sudetenland ceded to Germany; German occupation of Czechoslovakia.

Timeline

Glossary

ancien régime: The union of throne and altar that characterized the absolute monarch of France before 1789.

antipope: A putative head of the Roman Church not officially recognized as a successor to St. Peter and not numbered in the list of the papal succession.

Arditi: Italian elite assault troops of the First World War whose name was taken after 1919 by nationalists in the formation of bands of ex-soldiers and violent nationalists for political purposes. They were identified by their black shirts and daggers. After the Great War, they were also known as *squadristi*.

Assembly of Notables: In pre-revolutionary France, a meeting of the first two estates—the clergy and nobility—to advise the king.

assignats: The state bonds issued in 1790 by the Revolutionary government secured by the nationalization of the estates of the church.

canon law: The law of and governing the Roman Catholic Church.

Carbonari: "Charcoal burners" or Italian nationalist underground conspirators whose goal was to liberate Italy from the Austrians and establish an independent Italian state.

Chartist movement: A British reform movement during the 1830s and 1840s that collected signatures in a petition to Parliament to demand manhood suffrage, a secret ballot, annual elections, paid M.P.s, and equal constituencies.

comitatus: The band of privileged retainers in service to a barbarian chieftain.

concordat: A diplomatic treaty negotiated between the Roman Catholic Church and a government on issues of religious significance.

Corn Laws: The tariffs on imported grains in England repealed in 1846.

deism: A belief in a supreme being as first cause in the creation of a rational universe but with no fixed ecclesiastical or theological structure.

devotion moderna: The program of lay piety and learning derived from the teachings of Gerhard Groote in the Netherlands.

Directory (*Directoire*): Under the Constitution of 1795, the collective executive of five men who led France after the Terror and before Napoleon's 1799 coup.

empiricism: The scientific and philosophical system based upon the assessment and recognition of verifiable, observable evidence and sense experience to determine knowledge.

Estates General: The meeting of all three estates (clergy, nobility, and people) to advise the king in pre-revolutionary France.

excommunication: The exclusion of an individual from the sacraments because of crimes against the Church or religion.

Fasci: Bands of nationalist zealots in Italy, forming the early nucleus of the Fascist party under Mussolini. The name comes from the *fasces* or bundles of rods with axe heads carried by the *lictors* before a consul symbolizing the power to punish. Also, the bundled rods are symbolically stronger than individual faggots, indicating strength through unity and the subjection of the individual to the group: key Fascist ideological principles.

fief: The land held by a vassal with feudal obligations to his lord.

Frankfort Assembly: The parliament of the German-speaking territories of Europe that met for just over one year (May 1848–May 1849) that unsuccessfully worked towards German unification.

Freikorps: Bands of paramilitary nationalist veterans, unemployed and bitter over Germany's defeat in the First World War, who fought socialist and communist revolutionaries. Hitler recruited his earliest storm troopers from these groups.

German Confederation: A loose identification of German speaking states after the Congress of Vienna in 1815 to replace the Holy Roman Empire suppressed by Napoleon and lasting until the Prussian victory over Austria in 1866.

Girondins: A radical republican faction after the Revolution who wanted a more decentralized France (from the region of the Gironde, around Bordeaux, from which many of its leaders arose).

Huguenot: A French Protestant, usually a Calvinist.

humanism: The Renaissance revival of antiquity and its application to contemporary issues.

Imperial Diet: The advisory body representing the leading secular and ecclesiastical principalities and jurisdictions to the emperor in the Holy Roman Empire.

Index of Prohibited Books: Books which Catholics were prohibited from reading or possessing, first established in 1559.

indulgences: The documents available for purchase from the church in order to accelerate the release of souls from Purgatory.

intendants: Instituted by Richelieu, those royal officers responsible for fiscal and legal functions in their districts.

Jacobins: A radical republican faction in the French national assembly after the Revolution, arguing for the centralization of power (from the priory of St Jacques in Paris, which was granted to this faction as a meeting house).

Kulturkampf (culture war): The campaign against the Roman Catholic Church in the German Empire waged by Bismarck between approximately 1871 and 1883.

Les Politiques: The political theorists around Henri IV who advocated practical, rational compromise as solutions to national problems, such as the issue of uniformity in religion.

Luddites: Named after the fictitious Ned Ludd: workers during the industrial revolution in the early 19th century who sabotaged machinery or set fires in factories because they believed their handicraft employment had been lost to automated production.

mercantilism: The centralized regulation of trade and commerce to ensure that no profit would be lost to the nation.

morganatic: Describing a marriage in which a partner of noble or royal rank weds one who is of lower rank with the provision that neither the spouse of lower rank nor any children born of the marriage may lay claim to the position or property of the higher-ranking partner.

obscurantism: Opposition to free enquiry, rationalism, and—in particular—the Enlightenment.

Pan-Slavism: The 19th- and early 20th-century belief that all Slavic peoples are linked through a common culture, traditions, linguistic base, and orthodox religion, supported by imperial Russia as the only Slavic great power.

parlement: French law courts in major cities before the Revolution, with the Parlement of Paris having extraordinary authority and respect.

philosophe: A rationalist thinker or writer during the Enlightenment of the 18th century.

plebiscite: A vote by the qualified voters of a state in order to directly decide some important public question.

pocket borough: A Parliamentary constituency in Britain before the Reform Bill of 1832 in which the landlord could effectively appoint the M.P.

positivism: The theory derived in part from Auguste Comte that only science and verifiable truth should be used to guide philosophical, social, political, or economic action.

Puritans: The general term for English reformers who wished a complete break from Roman Catholic liturgy, practice, and symbols in the later 16th and 17th centuries.

Risorgimento: The "resurgence" or national unification movement in Italy from the age of Napoleon until the creation of a united Italian monarchy in 1861 and capture of Rome in 1870.

romantic movement: The literary and artistic movement beginning at the end of the 18th and lasting through the first decades of the 19th century, which emphasized subjective experience, emotion, and nature over pure reason,

rotten borough: A Parliamentary constituency in Britain before the Reform Bill of 1832 in which there were few—if any—electors.

Spartacists: Communist revolutionary bands, inspired by the Bolshevik revolution in Russia, who attempted to foment a similar uprising in Germany after the First World War. The name is taken from Spartacus, the leader of the slave revolt against the Romans in 73 B.C.

tax farming: The selling of the privilege during the ancien régime of monopolies to private investors to collect the taxes of particular regions for a fixed duration.

Triple Alliance: The alliance among Germany, Austria-Hungary, and Italy at the outbreak of the First World War.

Triple Entente: The alliance among Britain, France, and Russia at the outbreak of the First World War.

utilitarianism: The Enlightenment and liberal doctrine that argued that for something to be good it had to be useful to the greatest number possible.

vassal: A subject of a feudal lord who accepts land in return for service and military support.

Zollverein: The customs union of German-speaking territories established first by the Prussians in 1818 but expanding until 1866 to include almost all the German states.

Biographical Notes

Baboeuf, François "Gracchus" (1760–1797): Known as the Tribune, Baboeuf "Gracchus" (a designation that alludes to the famous Roman reformers, the Gracchi) was a French political journalist and dissenter in the period of the French Revolution. One of the first socialists, Baboeuf was arrested, tried, and convicted for his involvement with the Conspiracy of the Equals, which was aimed at provoking an armed uprising of the plebeian masses against the bourgeois regime of the Directory and establishing a revolutionary dictatorship as a transitional stage to pure democracy and egalitarian communism. According to common legend, upon hearing his sentence, Baboeuf attempted to kill himself with a self-made dagger but his guards saved him only to carry him off to the guillotine the next morning. He was remembered and revered by his followers long after his execution.

Bacon, Francis (1561–1626): English philosopher, historian, founder of empirical science, and politician elected to Parliament in 1584. Bacon is best known for the method of scientific inquiry called induction, which is the acquisition of knowledge through experimentation and observation, described in *Novum Organum* (1620). In 1621, Bacon was accused of bribery, found guilty, and dismissed from office. He was later pardoned but never resumed his political career, instead dedicating his last years to science.

Bentham, Jeremy (1748–1832): English writer, jurist, and a founder of liberalism. Bentham was the architect of utilitarianism, an ethical theory based on the principle of usefulness in which human actions are only judged valid if efficient in ensuring "the greatest good for the greatest number," described in *Deontology, or the Science of Morality* (1834). He supported the movement to reform Parliament, believing it necessary to extend the right to vote to all citizens, but nevertheless criticized the *Social Contract* of Jean-Jacques Rousseau as too radical. Bentham also supported women in their demands for equal rights and maintained that slavery, physical torture, and penalties for homosexuality were not consonant with human rights.

Bismarck, Otto von (1815–1898): Conservative Prussian politician and nobleman, who in 1861 became the minister-president of Germany and in 1867 the first chancellor of the North-German Confederation, overseeing the unification of Germany under Prussia in 1871 following the Franco-Prussian War. Bismarck was a practitioner of realpolitik, the Machiavellian political theory that advocated policies based on current necessity rather than ideological or moral convictions. Bismarck consequently adopted policies advocated by liberals, such as social legislation. He is remembered for his management of German unification through war and cynical diplomacy, as well as for his remark that "one day a great war will come out of some damned foolish thing in the Balkans."

Blanqui, Louis-Auguste (1805–1881): Blanqui was a socialist activist in post-Revolutionary France. He became the leader of several communist movements, such as the *Amis du peuple* and the *Société républicaine centrale*, as well as editing the radical Swiss journal *La patrie en danger*. Blanqui took part in most revolutionary events in France and spent more than 37 years of his life in prison. He was a radical atheist, believing that religion was one of the greatest weaknesses of humanity. Blanqui did not leave any substantial work but inspired many followers, including Marx, who nevertheless rejected his example as mere terrorism without "scientific" ideological content.

Bonaparte, Napoleon (1769–1821): Brilliant revolutionary general, first consul, and then emperor of the French as Napoleon I, (1804–1814). Napoleon was Corsican by birth but educated at the elite military academy in Paris. He rose to power during the years of the First French Republic by successfully campaigning against the enemies of Revolutionary France. In 1799, he overthrew the Directory in a coup that resulted in his becoming first consul, then first consul for life—in effect, military dictator. In 1804 he completed his acquisition of power through his coronation as emperor. His military campaigns initially defeated every major power on the Continent except Britain. However, his failures in Russia (1812) and Spain resulted in a vast coalition against France that defeated Napoleon in 1814. He abdicated the throne and was first exiled with honor to Elba, but his attempt to return to France (the Hundred Days) resulted in his second exile, this time to St. Helena in the South Atlantic, where he died in 1822.

Bright, John (1811–1889): British radical politician, Quaker, and a major figure in the Anti-Corn Law League, a movement for the abolition of tariffs on imported grains. After the Corn Laws were abolished in 1846, Bright continued to challenge the protectionist economic practices of the government as well as Britain's foreign policy. Bright received much literary and social recognition during his lifetime, although his pacifist religion disqualified him from high office.

Brunel, Isambard Kingdom (1806–1859): British engineer who oversaw the project of the first iron steamship, the *Great Eastern*, specifically designed to lay the first transatlantic telegraph cable. Brunel was also involved in the construction of both the Great Western Railway and the first permanent tunnel under the Thames. During the Crimean War in 1854, Brunel designed a military hospital in the Dardanelles, complete with an aqueduct, plumbing system, and railway to transport patients from the coast. Brunel is celebrated as one of the first comprehensive engineers, combining specialized knowledge with broad education, including classical studies and foreign languages.

Calvin, John (1509–1564): One of the most influential figures of the Protestant Reformation. A pastor and theologian, Calvin was born in France, the son of a lawyer. After converting to reformed religion, he fled to Basel, Switzerland in 1530. In 1536, Calvin was invited to Geneva to help reform the church in that city; in the same year he published his seminal theological work, *Institutes of the Christian Religion*. In this work Calvin developed his doctrine of predestination and salvation by the grace of God. Calvin's thought directly influenced the development of several branches of Protestantism, such as Puritanism and Presbyterianism.

Cavour, Camillo di (1810–1861): Italian statesman. As Prime Minister of the Kingdom of Piedmont-Sardinia, Cavour played a central role in the unification of Italy under the authority of the king of Piedmont, Victor Emmanuel II. Following unification in 1861, Cavour was made the Prime Minister of Italy, but he died soon afterwards. In addition to his political activities, he wrote important works on such diverse themes as taxation, agrarian development, economics, and railway construction.

Charlemagne (c. 747–814): Son of Pippin, King of the Franks, Charlemagne (or Charles the Great) expanded his kingdom into the first great European empire since the Romans. He was supported by the Catholic Church, campaigning against the pagan peoples of the North and East and converting them to Christianity. In the year 800 Charlemagne was crowned *Imperator Augustus*, the first Holy Roman Emperor, by Pope Leo III. Charlemagne encouraged the Carolingian Renaissance, a revival of knowledge under the patronage of the Church. He is also recognized as helping restore a common European identity after the collapse of Rome.

Charles I of England (1600–1649): The son of James VI of Scotland and I of England, Charles I became King of England, Scotland, and Ireland in March 1625. He believed in the divine right of kings, and struggled to subordinate Parliament to his will. Charles provoked the English Civil Wars (1642–1649) with his marriage to the Catholic Henrietta Maria of France, sympathy with conservative Anglican practices and theology, and his high-handed dealing with Parliament. Twice defeated in his campaigns against the forces of the Parliament, Charles was arrested, charged with high treason, and executed on January 30, 1649. His execution prompted the temporary abolition of the monarchy in England and the institution of the Commonwealth during the Interregnum, with the nation ruled by Oliver Cromwell as military dictator.

Charles V of Habsburg (1500–1558): King of Aragon from 1516 and Holy Roman Emperor from 1519, Charles was one of the most influential monarchs in the first half of the 16th century, ruling a united Spain, the Low Countries, the Empire, much of Italy, and the Indies—the greatest empire since Charlemagne. His reign was characterized by wars, particularly against the French king Francis I and against the Lutherans, as the Reformation began in Germany during his rule as Emperor. He also engaged in wars with the Ottoman Empire, averting the Turkish danger from Vienna and liberating Christian slaves in Tunis. Charles abdicated his many crowns in 1556, dividing his empire between his brother, who became Holy Roman Emperor, and his son, Philip, who became king of Spain, Naples, and Sicily, and ruler of the Indies. Charles spent the last months of his life in a monastery.

Colbert, Jean-Baptiste (1619–1683): The most prominent minister under Louis XIV. As a mercantilist, Colbert regulated imports, exports, and trade, centralizing economic activity. Under his system, France built a great navy and merchant fleet and facilitated the structure of absolutism through centralized policies at court. However, the French economy, both mercantile and agricultural, ultimately suffered from over-regulation and high taxation. Colbert still managed to pay for the exorbitant costs of Louis's wars and his new palace at Versailles, but weakened the financial position of the kingdom by failing to modernize the taxation system.

Columbus, Christopher (1451–1506): A famous navigator and explorer, Columbus was born into a middle-class family in Genoa. Having worked at sea and as a cartographer, Columbus calculated that the circumference of Earth was smaller than generally believed and thought Asia could be easily reached by sailing west across the Atlantic. He had difficulty funding his project because experienced navigators knew that Earth was in fact larger than Columbus suggested. Eventually he convinced Isabella of Castile and Ferdinand of Aragon to support his first voyage in 1492, resulting in his discovery of the Americas, which he claimed for their crowns. Three subsequent voyages followed, thus beginning the European conquest and colonization of the New World.

Comte, Auguste (1798–1857): French philosopher who founded of positivism and established sociology as an independent discipline. Positivism argues that knowledge should only be accepted as reliable if proven from sense experience. This theory, described in *The Course of Positive Philosophy* (1830) and *The System of Positive Politics* (1851–1854), was proposed by Comte as a remedy to social problems that France experienced since the Revolution. The ideal structure of society, he suggested, was a strict hierarchy in which the wealthy, educated bourgeoisie are at the top and entrusted with the government of the state and the welfare of the working class. He believed this system would be harmonious, functional, and self-regulating, not unlike the Newtonian laws of nature. Despite his orderly philosophical system, Comte himself was given to episodes of mental instability and susceptible to religious mysticism.

Corradini, Enrico (1865–1931): Corradini was an Italian poet and novelist and founder of the radical right-wing newspaper *Il Regno*, an antecedent to fascism. He was also a founder of the Italian Nationalist Party (*Associazione Nazionalista Italiana*) in 1910. Corradini argued that nations are defined socially, just as classes are; and his strident nationalism encouraged Italian imperialism and militarism. His speeches and journalism powerfully influenced nationalist extremists, intent on direct action and opposed to the liberal, bourgeois Italian state, and united in their hatred of socialists, internationalists, and pacifists. After the First World War, the Italian Nationalist Party led by Corradini merged with Mussolini's Italian fascist party.

Cortes, Hernando (1485–1547): A Spanish conquistador, Hernando Cortes was the leader of the expedition to Mexico that conquered the kingdom of the Aztecs. Settling first in Cuba, he served as a magistrate but in 1519 he funded an expedition to the mainland. In 1521, after a long campaign, Cortes managed to conquer Tenochtitlan, the capital city of the Aztec Empire for Spain. He was a violent, unattractive, greedy man, who was not popular with the colonial authorities in Spain; hence, his contribution to the Spanish crown was never adequately appreciated and he was denied the more prestigious title of Viceroy. Cortes died in Spain, embittered, requesting before his death that his remains be transported back to Mexico.

Cromwell, Oliver (1599–1658): Leader of the anti-royalist coalition in the English Civil War against King Charles I. A talented strategist and military innovator, he often defeated the royalists in battle and by 1648 emerged as victor. After the execution of Charles in 1649, Cromwell presided over the Commonwealth of England and was awarded by Parliament the title of Lord Protector. Ruling with no constitutional authority, effectively as military dictator, Cromwell expelled his critics from Parliament, abolished the House of Lords, and instituted a strict Puritan regime. After Cromwell's death, he was succeeded by his son, Richard, who was unable to maintain his father's position, given the forces arrayed against him. In 1660, the Stuart monarchy was restored and Oliver Cromwell's body was exhumed, hanged in chains, and beheaded.

Darwin, Charles (1809–1882): English naturalist, traveler, and biologist. Darwin was one of the first scientists to demonstrate that all living organisms evolve over time from common ancestors. His theory, developed in *On the Origin of Species* (1859), proved that the principle of evolution depended on natural selection. This theory illustrated how small variations in the offspring of any species offered greater or lesser opportunities for survival to produce their own descendents; over time, these small differences led to structural changes in the species themselves. In 1871, Darwin proposed the same theory for human evolution in *The Descent of Man*. While evolution was acknowledged as a demonstrable fact by most scientists after 1859, Darwin's work divided Europe between those more comfortable with traditional explanations for natural phenomena and those keen to embrace science.

Descartes, René (1596–1650): Frenchman who spent a good part of his life abroad, Descartes was a key figure in the scientific revolution, with important contributions in the fields of mathematics and philosophy. In mathematics, he invented the Cartesian coordinate system, which allows functions to be expressed as algebraic equations. His short treatise of 1637, *The Discourse on Method*, which defined scientific method and institutionalized the principle that phenomena had to be proven true before being accepted, offered an elegant and effective mechanism for the assessment of knowledge. His main contribution in philosophy was the method of radical skepticism, first formulated in his *Principles of Philosophy* (1644). According to this method, the only thing that does not require proof is the fact of our existence: We think, therefore we exist (*cogito ergo sum*). Descartes had an enormous influence on the mind of the West and was a founder of the Enlightenment.

Diderot, Denis (1713–1784): French writer, philosopher, art critic, and playwright. Diderot is known for his important contributions to literature and letters, but his editing of the great *Encyclopédie* with Jean d'Alembert is his greatest contribution to the mind of Europe, making the ideas of the Enlightenment available to anyone who had access to its volumes of plates and text. He wrote over 1,000 entries personally and assigned many others to the greatest experts of his day, such as Voltaire, Rousseau, Turgot, and Buffon. Diderot believed powerfully in the centrality of free speech and a free press to disseminate correct information for rational, enlightened action in every aspect of life. Although he had originally trained for the Church, he became extremely anti-clerical and hostile to organized religion. He was supported by Catherine the Great of Russia, who bought his library, but mostly lived from his writing.

Disraeli, Benjamin (1804–1881): Popular novelist and leading figure of the British Conservative Party after 1844 and the 42nd Prime-Minister of Britain, elected in 1868 and between the years 1874 and 1880. Of Jewish heritage, Disraeli converted to Anglicanism in his youth. He was a favorite Prime Minister of Queen Victoria and skillfully advanced the goals of the British Empire abroad, such as the acquisition of the Suez Canal that greatly shortened the distance between Britain and India. His domestic policy broadened the appeal of the Conservative Party from its narrow, landed, aristocratic base, making it a real alternative to the Liberals in a time of wider franchise, a policy Disraeli supported. After leaving politics he was raised to the peerage as Lord Beaconsfield.

Dreyfus, Alfred (1859–1935): A French artillery officer of Jewish descent, Alfred Dreyfus was accused in 1894 of treason and spying for the Germans. Despite contrary evidence, Dreyfus was convicted, publicly stripped of his army rank, and sentenced to life imprisonment on Devil's Island in French Guiana (1895). Soon, however, many began to doubt the fairness of the trial. An investigation implicated another suspect. Many liberal politicians, intellectuals, and writers, such as Georges Clemenceau, Emile Zola, and Anatole France, demanded his release, accusing the military establishment and the right wing political parties and press of fabricating the evidence to feed anti-Semitism. Their campaign was successful. In 1899 Dreyfus was officially pardoned, released from prison, and exonerated by a military commission.

Ebert, Friedrich (1871–1925): Friedrich Ebert was a leader of the German Social Democratic Party. He was leader of the socialist majority in the Reichstag in 1918 at the end of the First World War and given the responsibility of providing some measure of functioning government for the defeated Germans. Despite his affiliation with the socialists, he only reluctantly accepted the proclamation of the republic in Germany in 1918 and his election under the Weimar constitution as its first president. With the breakdown of civil order and Bolshevik rebellions occurring across the nation, Ebert used the Freikorps to suppress the "Spartacist" uprisings, seeing these nationalist thugs increasingly favorably as the only force prepared to protect Germany against a Marxist revolution.

Elizabeth I of England (1533–1603): Daughter of Henry VIII and Ann Boleyn, Elizabeth I of England was the last monarch of the Tudor dynasty. She succeeded Mary I on the throne, ending a decade of political and religious turmoil that had followed Henry's death. Implementing sensitive and pragmatic policies in religion, she managed in 1559 to maneuver England to a moderate Protestant confession and church structure that would not alienate conservatives. Elizabeth's reign saw the growing importance of England as a naval and imperial power, defeating the Spanish Armada in 1588, and staking claim to the future British colonies in North America and the Caribbean. Her reign was also one of great cultural richness, establishing the Elizabethan Age as one of the greatest in English history. Elizabeth never married and was succeeded by James VI of Scotland, the son of her cousin Mary, Queen of Scots, whom she reluctantly had executed for plotting against her.

Engels, Friedrich (1820–1895): Friedrich Engels was a German political theorist and one of the founders of Communism. In 1848 he co-authored with Karl Marx *The Communist Manifesto* and later edited and oversaw the posthumous publication of the last volumes of Marx's most important work, *Das Kapital* (1867–1894). Born into a mill-owning family in the textile town of Barmen in Germany, Engels, as a university student, developed an interest in the philosophy of G. W. F. Hegel as expounded by the Young Hegelians and became persuaded that the logical consequence of Hegelian dialectic was communism. Engels moved from Germany to England in 1842, where he worked as a manager in one of his family's factories. In 1844 he published *The Condition of the Working Class in England*, which suggested that the only way the working class could improve their desperate conditions was through socialism. Despite Marx's difficult and imperious personality, Engels remained loyal to him and worked, often unacknowledged, at his side until Marx's death.

Erasmus, Desiderius (1469–1536): Erasmus was the most eminent humanist scholar and theologian of the Renaissance. He was born in Holland, the illegitimate son of a priest. His parents died while Erasmus was still a boy, but he was nevertheless sent to an excellent school run by the Brethren of the Common Life. At a young age, under pressure from his guardians, Erasmus took vows as an Augustinian canon, but later received dispensation from his monastic vows directly from the pope. He is known for his translation of the New Testament from the original Greek and for his literary works such as *The Praise of Folly*. Initially Erasmus showed sympathy with Luther's revolution in 1517 and agreed with many of Luther's assessments of the problems in the Church. However, Erasmus parted company over his division of Christendom into separate religions, a dichotomy that Erasmus deplored, and over the principle of free will, which unlike Luther, Erasmus believed was essential to human dignity.

Ferdinand and Isabella (1452–1516) and (1451–1504): In a dynastic marriage in 1479, Ferdinand II of Aragon and Isabella I of Castile united their kingdoms and prepared to integrate the Iberian peninsula into a single Christian kingdom shared with Portugal. To accomplish this, they began a crusade to conquer those parts of Spain still under Muslim rule. After successfully driving out the Moors from Grenada in 1492, the Catholic monarchs issued a decree ordering the expulsion of the Jews and Moors from Spain, although those who chose to convert to Christianity were permitted to stay. The Inquisition was given great power to investigate non-Christians; within a short period of time the Iberian Peninsula changed from one of the most religiously tolerant places in Europe to among the least tolerant. It was also during their reign that Columbus discovered the New World, sailing under their flag.

Fourier, Charles (1772–1837): Fourier was a French philosopher who developed models of utopian socialism, believing that society would greatly benefit from cooperation and "scientific" organization. He proposed the creation of communities called *phalanstaries* (phalanxes) housed in four-level apartment complexes where all citizens were accommodated according to a predetermined hierarchy. Work was assigned based on the interests and desires of the individual men and women and compensated according to their contributions, although a graduated income tax would reduce everyone to an essential equality, something Fourier saw as necessary for harmony. Fourier influenced socialist ideas outside the Marxist mainstream and inspired a movement of *Fourierists* in America who established phalanxes throughout the country, such as Utopia, in Ohio. Fourier is also credited with having coined the word "feminism."

Franz-Joseph I of Austria (1830–1916): Franz-Joseph I von Habsburg was the emperor of Austria (after 1867 Austria-Hungary), ruling for 68 years over this vast territory. His reign was marked by the weakening of the Austrian empire occasioned by the nationalist movements that detached his central and southern Italian provinces from his empire and which suffered ignominious defeat at the hands of the Prussians during the period of German unification. Besides being scarred by political and military failure, Franz-Josef's personal life was tragic, with the murder-suicide of his son, the crown-prince Rudolf and Rudolph's mistress, the assassination of his estranged wife, the Empress Elizabeth ("Sissi") in Geneva and, more ominously, of his nephew and heir, Franz-Ferdinand, in Sarajevo. Franz-Joseph lived long enough to preside over the outbreak of hostilities in 1914 but died before the disintegration of the huge dynastic empire constructed through the centuries by his ancestors.

Galilei, Galileo (1564–1642): Italian physicist, astronomer, philosopher, and mathematician, Galileo Galilei is recognized today as a founder of modern science. He invented and used a telescope to observe the Moon, planets, and stars, making a series of important scientific discoveries. Galileo was also the inventor of experiential physics, replacing the speculative metaphysics of Aristotle and building the foundation for mechanics. During his lifetime he was an active supporter of Copernicus's theory of the heliocentric structure of the universe proposed in the previous century, and consequently came into conflict with the Catholic Church, which insisted on scripture, the ancients, and imperfect observation to promulgate belief in a geocentric universe. He was accused of heresy and warned to stop teaching Copernicus's theory; but after publishing his famous *Dialogue Concerning the Two Chief World Systems* in 1632, he was tried as a contumacious heretic and ordered either to recant his views or to be burned. Old, almost blind, and exhausted, Galileo recanted, but famously noted *sotto voce*, "and yet it [the earth] moves."

Garibaldi, Giuseppe (1807–1882): Italian nationalist, military adventurer, and political figure born in Genoa, the son of sailor and a sailor himself. In 1833 Garibaldi joined the Carbonari, a secret nationalist society whose main goal was to liberate Italy from the Austrians. He participated in an unsuccessful insurrection in 1834 and had to flee, first to France and then to South America where he joined the Uruguayan Civil War as the leader of an Italian squad. He later returned to Italy and took part in the Revolution of 1848 in Rome against the pope. With the suppression of the Roman Republic in 1849 by French troops, Garibaldi again fled into hiding. But in 1860, he led a band of 1,000 red-shirted followers to Sicily, where they defeated the forces of the Bourbons of Naples and then crossed the Straits of Messina to the mainland and drove the king into exile. Garibaldi then ceded the Kingdom of the Two Sicilies to King Victor Emmanuel. Opposed to the continued rule of the pope in Rome, Garibaldi attempted to use volunteers to capture the city and the remaining papal territories in 1862, an adventure not supported by the king. The Italian regular army stopped Garibaldi's band at Aspromonte where he was wounded. Despite this event, Garibaldi continued to fight and work for the complete unification of Italy, fighting the Austrians in 1866 and agitating for the capture of Rome.

Gladstone, William Ewart (1809–1898): Four times Prime Minister of Great Britain. Having begun his career as a Tory, in 1846 he followed Robert Peel in becoming Liberal-Conservative. As leader of the Liberal Party from 1867, Gladstone was elected Prime Minister for the first time in the following year, establishing himself as the political rival of the conservative statesman, Benjamin Disraeli. Gladstone is known for his lengthy campaign for home-rule for Ireland, as well as for his contribution to the national elementary school program and reform of the justice system and the civil service.

Gobineau, Comte Arthur de (1816–1882): French social theorist, writer, and historian, who is credited with the articulation of modern racial theory. Having served for a short period of time as chancellor to Alexis de Tocqueville and as a diplomat, Gobineau eventually established himself as a writer of pamphlets and political publicist. He developed a theory that social order and culture are predetermined by race, arguing that physiological and mental distinctions between white, yellow, and black races are natural barriers that cause racial degeneration if transgressed. Thus Gobineau opposed colonialism, claiming that it would endanger the white race by exposing it to possible miscegenation with "inferior" races. Although his *An Essay on the Inequality of the Human Races* (1853–1855) was not widely influential in his own time, it was later appropriated by the Nazis and others in the formulation of their own racial theories.

Gustavus Adolphus of Sweden (1594–1632): King of Sweden from 1611–1632. A talented diplomat and general, Gustavus Adolphus was able to make Sweden one of the most powerful states in the world. He reformed the navy and army and employed the latest technology in military equipment and tactics. During the Thirty Years War, he became the leader of the Protestant alliance against the Catholic Habsburgs and waged successful campaigns against them until confronted by the imperial army under Wallenstein. In 1632, after leading his troops into battle with acts of heroic bravery, Gustavus Adolphus was killed at the Battle of Lutzen against Wallenstein's army. Besides his reputation as a soldier and devout Protestant monarch, he was a supporter of the arts, science, and culture, founding the University of Uppsala. At his death, his heir was his very young daughter, Queen Christina of Sweden.

Henri IV of France (1553–1610): Also Henry of Navarre, King Henri IV effectively ended the French Wars of Religion (1562–1598). During the early years of his life, Henri was a leader of the Protestant (Huguenot) cause. With the assassination of the Guises under Henri III, Henry assumed the throne when that king was assassinated in 1589. Despite his conversion to Catholicism, he protected the Protestants to cement his claim to the throne. In 1598 he issued the tolerant Edict of Nantes, which secured the liberties and property of Protestants in France. He was one of the most popular and successful monarchs of his age, unusually tolerant and concerned for the welfare of his people. He followed practical political advice from his advisers, who put the well-being of his kingdom above all other considerations, including religion. In 1610, Henri IV was assassinated by a Catholic fanatic, François Ravaillac, leaving the throne to his young son, Louis XIII.

Henry VIII of England (1491–1547): Henry Tudor became King of England in 1509. Described as an ideal Renaissance prince at the beginning of his reign, he soon fell into despair at his failure to secure a male heir to protect the dynasty and keep England safe from a renewal of civil war. Henry struggled to annul his first marriage to Catherine of Aragon by seeking papal approval through the intercession of his chief minister, Cardinal Wolsey. Pope Clement VII, largely under the control of Catherine's nephew, Charles V, would not grant an annulment. Henry then set in motion a chain of events that led to England's break with Catholicism and to the consummation of his short-lived marriage to Anne Boleyn. This marriage, which produced a daughter, Elizabeth, ended with Anne's beheading in 1536. Four more marriages followed, the third of which, to Jane Seymour, produced the desired male heir, the future Edward VI. Henry's reform of the Church consisted mostly of appropriating the power of the papacy and the property of the monasteries for the crown. The Anglican Church, like Henry himself, remained conservative in theology and maintained many Catholic practices. However, his nationalization of the Roman Church in England greatly strengthened the power of Parliament, as reform occurred through Parliamentary statute, managed by his able chief minister, Cromwell.

Hobbes, Thomas (1588–1679): English political theorist and scientist. The son of a cleric, Hobbes was well educated and served as tutor to aristocratic families, undertaking with one of his pupils a grand tour that put him in direct contact with classical thought on the Continent. He subsequently relocated to Paris where he moved in scientific circles, adopting a materialist, rationalist perspective. The English civil war crystallized his thought, which increasingly rejected the divine arguments of both the Puritans and the royalists. Instead, in 1651 he published *Leviathan*, which postulated a secular notion of sovereignty based on a contract between ruler and subjects. The contract was required to reduce the horror and violence in the state of nature where the strong preyed upon the weak. But once the contract was made, it was indissoluble as subjects had freely abrogated their right to rebel. One of the seminal works of English political theory, *Leviathan* alienated both the Parliamentarians and the royalists. Hobbes sought obscurity, although his book was to influence subsequent political thought greatly, inspiring Locke and Rousseau to respond to his theory of contract later in his century and the next.

Hus, Jan (c. 1370–1415): A Bohemian (Czech) preacher, theologian, and philosopher, Jan Hus objected to many of the practices of the Catholic Church, which he argued were not based upon scripture. He also questioned the wealth of the Church, the injunction against vernacular scripture, and other elements of Roman Christianity. Hus was seen as both a theological heretic and a popular Czech leader opposed to an entrenched, largely German, episcopacy in Bohemia during the chaotic years of the Great Schism. The king of Bohemia and the Holy Roman Emperor, Sigismund summoned the Council of Constance where he invited Hus to appear before it, with clear promises of safe conduct. Nevertheless, in 1415 Hus was accused of heresy by the antipope John XXIII and burned at the stake with two of his closest disciples. His popularity among the Czechs in Bohemia, however, did not abate; indeed, his execution prompted the Hussite Wars (1419–1434) and the Hussite Reformation movement.

Huxley, Thomas (1825–1895): English zoologist, and one of the greatest advocates of Darwin's theory of evolution, nicknamed as a result "Darwin's Bulldog." Huxley's scientific interests lay in the field of comparative anatomy, in which he sought to find clues for the evolutionary development of organisms including humans, a subject he famously debated at Oxford with Richard Owen. Huxley strongly believed that science and reason must operate separately from religion and faith. It was in this context that Huxley coined the term agnosticism.

Kossuth, Lajos (Louis) (1802–1894): Hungarian politician, jurist, and a leader of the Hungarian Revolution of 1848–1849, serving as Governor-President of Hungary. Having launched a political and military campaign against the rule of the Austrian Habsburgs as kings of Hungary, Kossuth initially succeeded in separating Hungary from the Habsburg crown. Unfortunately, his policies towards the non-Magyar minorities alienated those groups who believed they enjoyed greater freedom under the Austrians. The peasants on the great landed estates of the Hungarian nobility feared their landlords once the protection of Austrian law was removed. Thus, an army led by a Croatian noble invaded Hungary and defeated Kossuth, who fled into a long exile during which he continued to agitate for Hungarian independence. This was largely realized in the 1867 with the admission of Hungary to equal participation in the Austro-Hungarian Empire.

Lenin, Vladimir (1870–1924): Vladimir Ilyich Lenin (born Ulyanov) was the principal figure of the Russian Bolshevik Revolution of 1917. His life had been dedicated to Marxist revolutionary activity both in Russia and during his exile. Smuggled back into Russia by the Germans to foment revolution and perhaps drive Russia from the war, Lenin overthrew the liberal democrats who came to power after the first insurrection caused the abdication of the czar. This liberal government under Kerensky, however, intended to pursue the war, and Lenin had promised peace and bread. The subsequent "October Revolution" (November 7, 1917, Gregorian calendar) resulted in Lenin becoming the first leader of the newly declared "State of the Soviets." Soon after the Revolution, Lenin authorized the "Red Terror," which resulted in the imprisonment of his opponents and the mass execution of the *kulaks* (wealthy farmers). Having survived two assassination attempts, Lenin suffered a stroke in 1922 and retired. He spent the last years of his life worried about the bureaucratization of the regime and expressing concern over the increasing power of Joseph Stalin, his future successor.

Locke, John (1632–1704): English educator, political theorist, and a founder of empiricism. Influential in the development of modern epistemology, Locke argued in *An Essay Concerning Human Understanding* that human beings are born without any inborn knowledge (*tabula rasa*), denying both Cartesian and Christian epistemology. Knowledge, Locke claimed, is acquired through sense experience, which can be structured and taught to all children. Differences among men, then, were the result of varying education and experience, rather than intrinsic qualities of birth. His *Second Treatise of Civil Government* (1690) is one of the most important political texts of all time. It took Hobbes's contract theory and modified it by arguing that all humans are born with inalienable rights to life, liberty, and happiness, which cannot be taken from them without their consent or that of their representatives. If any government attempts to infringe on these basic human rights, citizens have the right to rebel, as the contract had been broken. Although written in part as a response to the Glorious Revolution, Locke's text soon became a fundamental statement of Liberal principle.

Louis Napoleon Bonaparte (Napoleon III) of France (1808–1873): Nephew of Napoleon I, president of the French Republic (1848–1852), and the Emperor of the French between 1852 and 1870. Although elected president of the second republic after the overthrow of Louis-Philippe, he effected a coup and became dictator, and in 1852 emperor, a position legalized by a referendum. Ten years into his reign, Napoleon III gradually restored personal and political freedoms, a process that culminated in the Liberal Constitution of 1870, which granted legislative power to the Chamber of Deputies. His foreign policy was ambitious, fighting the Russians in the Crimean War and the Austrians to help free Italy from their rule. In 1870 he was maneuvered by Bismarck into declaring war on Prussia, resulting in the devastating defeat at Sedan, where he and 100,000 of his troops were captured. The empire disintegrated and he fled into exile in Britain.

Louis XIV of France (1638–1715): King of France and Navarre from 1643. With the help of able ministers, Louis XIV perfected the practice of absolute monarchy, making the crown independent of any control. His reign, particularly the first half, reflected the economic, military, and cultural dominance of France on the Continent. His expenditures, such as the building of his vast new palace at Versailles, and his conduct of almost incessant wars eventually drained the treasury and exposed the crown to serious debt. His abrogation of the tolerant Edict of Nantes in 1685 drove many of his skilled subjects into exile. Nevertheless, his reign represented a Golden Age of French influence in culture and manufacturing.

Loyola, Ignatius of (1491–1556): Ignatius of Loyola was a Spanish soldier who in 1521 underwent a religious conversion, subsequently becoming a hermit and a priest. In 1540, Loyola founded the Society of Jesus, or the Jesuit Order, which was to play a major role in the Counter-Reformation. He provided the society with a constitution and a manual, the *Spiritual Exercises*, a collection of meditations, prayers, and mental exercises intended to help his followers discover God's will and follow it. His order centered on three functions: preaching, teaching, and missionary activity. It was largely as a result of the work of the Jesuits that Catholicism was able to withstand the attacks of the Protestants, return many to the Roman confession, and convert the inhabitants of newly contacted lands to the Catholic religion. Loyola was beatified after his death and canonized in 1622.

Luther, Martin (1483–1546): German monk, theologian, instigator of the European Reformation, and founder of Lutheranism. In 1517, Luther nailed his Ninety-Five Theses to the Castle Church door in Wittenberg to challenge the sale of indulgencies, claiming that salvation is a gift from God received by grace through faith in Christ. His theology put great emphasis on the Bible as the direct source of divine knowledge, motivating Luther to translate the Bible from Latin into German. In 1521, Luther was excommunicated by the Church and seen as a significant danger by the Emperor Charles V. His message was widely disseminated through printing and about half of Germany converted, including princes and cities that were able to acquire the property of the Church and exercise some control over what had previously been an independent jurisdiction. His personal revolt resulted in the division of Christendom into many, often warring sects, a situation that would lead to over a century of bloodshed.

Malthus, Thomas (1766–1834): British clergyman and scholar, widely known for his demographic theory that uncontrolled population growth will be regularly checked by natural disasters or famine (Malthusian Crisis). Malthus developed this idea as a challenge to the Enlightenment belief that society is constantly improving and through rational management the miseries of the past and present can in future be overcome. He claimed that the population of such a society would quickly outgrow its natural resources, as food increases only arithmetically while population grows geometrically. Thus Malthus concluded that famine would result if there were no war, malnutrition, and/or disease. His ideas greatly influenced the economic and social principles of the 19th century as well as stimulating Darwin to write *On the Origin of Species*.

Marx, Karl (1818–1883): A German philosopher, economist, and political journalist, Karl Marx was the major theorist of communism and socialism. After his education in Germany, he fled to Belgium where he was associated with the Communist League, for which in 1848 he and Friedrich Engels jointly composed *The Communist Manifesto*. Marx later moved to London, where he worked on his longest study, *Das Kapital*, again with Engels. Marx applied Hegelian dialectic to the "scientific" study of history to produce dialectical materialism, in which each dominant economic system produced its opposite, which then challenged it to produce a new theory. This process would continue until the ultimate—and he thought necessary—victory of socialism, after which the state would wither away, following the dictatorship of the proletariat. Although not an activist himself, Marx generated a large and widespread following across the continent among those who wished to improve the conditions of the industrial working class. Ultimately, however, much to Marx's disgust, most of these disciples chose to work within the legal framework of political parties or union organizations rather than to foment revolution, a required step for Marx.

Mazarin, Cardinal Jules (1602–1661): Italian cleric and diplomat who became a favorite of the Queen of France, Anne of Austria, after the death of her husband, Louis XIII. As the successor to Cardinal Richelieu as the king's chief minister, Mazarin effectively served as regent until Louis XIV came of age. He was skillful in controlling the aristocratic reaction to the policies of Richelieu during the royal minority and managed to contain the Frondes until the young king could exercise his authority. Mazarin was a great collector of art, books, and jewels, and was, unlike Richelieu, ambitious for personal wealth and for his family.

Mazzini, Giuseppe (1805–1872): Italian politician, patriot, writer, and philosopher, who played an important role in the struggle for the unification of Italy and in the movement for the liberal reform of politics. In 1831, while in France, Mazzini became the founder of the revolutionary movement Young Italy, which aspired to unite Italy and to liberate it from Austrian rule. In 1833, he organized an unsuccessful attack on the kingdom of Piedmont, after which he became persona non grata in Italy, France, and later Switzerland. Mazzini continued to take part in all revolutionary events in Italy during and after 1848, despite living in exile or in hiding. An uncompromising republican, he refused to participate in the parliamentary government that was established under the monarchy of the House of Savoy following Italian independence (1861). Mazzini was nevertheless rightly identified as one of the founders of modern Italy.

Mehmed (Mohammed) the Conqueror (1432–1481): Sultan of the Ottoman Empire between 1451 and 1481. Mehmed brilliantly captured Constantinople in 1453, putting an end to the Byzantine Empire. He then embarked on a series of expansionist wars, conquering much of Asia

Minor and the Balkans as far as Belgrade. A master of many languages, Mehmed was also interested in philosophy and poetry and patronized the arts and sciences. After conquering Constantinople, Mehmed amalgamated the old Byzantine administration into the Ottoman state and implemented many social and educational reforms, including support for schools and universities.

Metternich, Klemens von (1773–1859): Austrian diplomat and statesman, Metternich became a foreign minister of the Austrian Empire in 1809 after Napoleon's capture of Vienna, enjoying this office for the next 30 years. In his role as chief minister of the Habsburgs, he exercised great independence and control of most aspects of Austrian policy. He was a major figure in the negotiations before and during the Congress of Vienna (1814–1815), called to settle the many issues that arose from the Napoleonic and Revolutionary Wars. His policy, considered a prototype of modern foreign policy management and diplomatic practice, succeeded both in reintegrating France into the fraternity of Europe monarchies and imposing a very conservative regime on most of the Continent, particularly in Austria. The Revolution of 1848 drove him into exile, from which he returned to Austria in 1851 to live in retirement on his estates.

Mill, John Stuart (1806–1873): English philosopher and political theorist who profoundly influenced the shape of 19th-century British thought and political discourse. Supporting the freedom of the individual against the unlimited control of the state, Mill developed the harm principle: "the only purpose for which power can be rightfully exercised over any member of a civilized community, against his will, is to prevent harm to others." Mill advocated utilitarianism and empiricism in logic and mathematics, as well as social and political theory. Believing that the franchise should be as broad as possible, he strongly supported the Parliamentary reform bills and thought that political responsibility would reduce the threat of rebellion and irresponsibility amongst the poor. He was a spokesman for humane policies in prisons and in the empire and was a powerful and vocal advocate for the rights of women to enjoy full citizenship and personal freedom.

Montesquieu, Charles-Louis de Secondat, Baron de (1689–1755): French political thinker of the Enlightenment who articulated the theory of the separation of powers that influenced the first French and the American constitutions in his most important work, *De l'esprit des lois* (1748). Montesquieu proposed that the monarchy, the aristocracy, and the commons operate as mutual checks and balances, augmented by the existence of an independent judiciary and administrative structure—a theory he derived from his observation of the English Parliamentary system. Montesquieu, a social conservative, also argued that change had to be natural and organic, arising from the traditions and contexts of states or regions rather than imposed. He was a powerful opponent of the ancien régime, as he believed that absolutism was unnatural since it failed to allow for authorities outside the crown and could not respond to local traditions. Moreover, Montesquieu was an active politician, which again separated him from many of the other theorists of the 18th century. He inherited the seat of Bordeaux in the French Parlement and participated in the aristocratic reaction to Louis XIV's absolutism occasioned by the minority of Louis XV.

More, Thomas (1478–1535): English statesman, scholar, and writer, Thomas More was educated as a lawyer, but as a young man seriously considered a monastic life to fulfill his religious beliefs. He succeeded Cardinal Wolsey as Lord Chancellor to Henry VIII at the time of his separation from the Catholic Church. An uncompromising Catholic, More opposed both Luther's Reformation and Henry's decision to divorce Catherine of Aragon, refusing to sign the Act of Supremacy of 1534 that declared the king the Supreme Head of the Church of England. He resigned his office and although he committed no crime, his silent hostility to Henry's policies and to Henry's second marriage was seen as treason against the king. More was arrested, imprisoned, and eventually executed on July 6, 1535. Besides his political activity, he was one of England's leading Christian humanists, a close friend of Erasmus, and the author of one of Europe's most universally popular books, *Utopia*, published in 1516.

Mussolini, Benito (1883–1945): Benito Mussolini was an Italian journalist, agitator, and politician who became the leader of the Italian Fascist Party and first, prime minister, then dictator (duce), of Italy from 1922 to 1943. Mussolini was a leading figure in the creation of fascism, shifting his allegiance from the socialists—whose newspaper he edited—to the nationalist cause after the outbreak of World War I. He became a zealous nationalist and organizer of black-shirted thugs who fought street battles with socialists in the chaotic years after the end of the war. Supported by middle-class and wealthy Italians, the Fascists promised order and protection from a communist revolution. In 1922 Mussolini led his followers in a march on Rome. Rather than declare martial law in the face of this throng, the king asked Mussolini to form the government. Soon after, Italian liberal democracy was dismantled, resulting in a one-party dictatorship under Mussolini. In 1940 Mussolini led Italy into World War II on the side of the Axis powers. Following the Allied invasion of Italy in 1943, Mussolini was deposed and imprisoned. Freed by German soldiers, he established a fascist government in the north of Italy, but, threatened by the allied and partisan advance, tried to flee, only to be captured and executed, together with his mistress, Clara Petacci.

Newton, Isaac (1643–1727): Greatest English mathematician of his generation, Newton laid the foundation for differential and integral calculus, and his work on optics and gravitation made him one of the greatest scientists the world has ever known. In 1687 he published his *Philosophiae Naturalis Principia Mathematica*, one of the most influential books in the history of science. His description of the forces that drive the universe altered the perspective of many Europeans: They no longer believed themselves subject to an active and interfering God but, rather, inhabitants of a universe operating according to rational, comprehensible laws of nature. Newton was hardly an atheist, but he established science as the method for addressing the problems of nature and thus, by extension, mankind. Greatly honored in his life, Newton was buried in Westminster Abbey.

Nicholas II of Russia (1868–1918): Nicholas II Romanov was the last Russian czar before the Bolshevik Revolution of 1917 which overthrew the monarchy. Nicholas remains a controversial figure because of his resistance to social and political reforms. Nicholas presided over the humiliating defeat of Russia during the Russo-Japanese war of 1905 and the subsequent slaughter of peaceful petitioners in front of his palace that same year. He provided little if any support for the increasingly popular liberal constitutionalism arising after 1905 among the urban educated elites and even some nobles, preferring to maintain his autocracy. Russia suffered terribly during the First World War, and under this stress the state collapsed. The first Russian revolution established a liberal provisional government and provoked the czar's abdication. The subsequent Bolshevik Revolution of October 1917 saw Nicholas and his family imprisoned. In 1918 they were murdered under the order of Lenin.

Owen, Robert (1771–1858): Robert Owen was an English social reformer and mill owner who became greatly concerned about the condition of the industrial working class in his factories. He sought ways to improve their lives through the organization of social, economic, medical, and educational services in company facilities operated as cooperatives. He began experimenting with the cotton mills of New Lanark, Scotland, but his partners and other industrialists grew hostile to the expense and inefficiencies these experiments entailed, despite initial strong support from religious and social leaders. Eventually he sold these mills and tried his social theories in America, establishing the New Harmony community in Indiana. This community was designed to be self-sufficient, with the workers growing their own food, making their own clothes, and operating their shops and eventually becoming self-governing. The experiment proved a failure once again, although it had a profound influence on American utopians. Owen returned to England to put his energy and his wealth into the trade union movement, believing that political action by and for the workers was the only realistic solution to the social problems he had identified.

Pearson, Karl (1857–1936): British mathematician and a founder of the discipline of mathematical statistics. Pearson spent most of his career trying to apply mathematics and statistics to biological problems, becoming a supporter of the controversial science of eugenics defined by Francis

Galton—whose biography he wrote. Pearson became increasingly interested in developing mathematical methods for studying the processes of heredity and evolution and from 1911 to 1933 held the Galton chair of eugenics at the University of London. From 1893–1912 he wrote 18 papers entitled *Mathematical Contribution to the Theory of Evolution*, which contained his most valuable work. His *Grammar of Science* (London 1892) was recommended by Einstein. His commitment to eugenics, however, resulted in his advocating wars against "inferior" races and the acceptance of "natural" deaths among the weak and infirm as a means to avoid diluting the race. He was also vehemently opposed to colonization and became, ironically, a committed socialist and freethinker.

Petrarch, Francesco (1304–1374): A prominent Italian poet, Francesco Petrarch (or Petrarca) is commonly regarded as the father of the Italian humanism—an intellectual movement associated with the revival of ancient Roman and Greek literature that began in the 14th century. Born of an exiled Florentine notary in Arezzo, Petrarch grew up and was schooled in Avignon, before studying law at Bologna and returning to Italy. He became famous through his love poems dedicated to Laura and his wide correspondence. Petrarch was highly critical of the learning of his own age, criticizing scholasticism, the dominant method of learning in the universities, as arid and useless, focusing too much on logic and abstract and abstruse subjects. Instead, he looked for guidance to the ancients in his learning, especially the Roman statesman, philosopher, and rhetorician, Marcus Tullius Cicero.

Philip II of Spain (1527–1598): Son and co-heir of Charles V of Habsburg, the Holy Roman Emperor. In 1554 he was crowned the King of Naples and Sicily. Then in 1556, through his marriage to Mary I of England, he became the King of England and Ireland. That same year, after the renunciation of the throne by his father in 1556, he became King of Spain. He was also ruler of the Low Countries and King of Portugal from 1580. Philip inherited his father's leadership of the Catholic cause in Europe, warring against the Calvinists in the Netherlands and sending the Armada against England in 1588. He benefited from the rich treasures coming from the Spanish dominions in the New World and sustained, as a result, a vigorous foreign and military policy.

Pizarro, Francisco (c. 1475–1541): Pizarro was a Spanish conquistador who conquered the Incan Empire and founded Lima, the capital of Peru. In 1502, Pizarro sailed from Spain for the New World and in 1513 accompanied Vasco Nunez de Balboa in his crossing of Panama to the Pacific Coast. In 1519, Pizarro was granted the position of magistrate of the then recently founded City of Panama. Accounts of the gold-rich territory of the Incas that lay further west in South America, the legendary Eldorado, caught Pizarro's attention and prompted several expeditions to find and conquer the Incas. The third of these expeditions, in 1533, proved to be successful, as Pizarro captured Cusco, the capital of the Incan Empire, and executed the ruler Atahualpa. A brutal and violent man, Pizarro was killed in a conspiracy against him in Peru in 1541.

Pope Pius IX (1792–1878): The longest reigning pope in history, reigning from 1846 until his death, leaving a significant, and controversial, legacy. At the beginning of his reign Pius introduced social and economic reforms into the Papal States, which in general prompted liberalization of the backward territory. Later, however, as a consequence of the 1848–1849 Roman revolution that drove him from his state, he turned conservative, resisting the unification of Italy, as well as refusing secular and liberal reforms. In his *Syllabus of Errors*, a document issued in 1864, Pius condemned concepts such as freedom of religion and freedom of thought, as well as the separation of church and state. When the army of a united Italy captured Rome by force in 1870, Pius became the Prisoner of the Vatican, demanding Catholics not recognize the secular, liberal Italian state but follow his example and disassociate themselves from it. Theologically, his contributions were to make the belief in the Immaculate Conception of the Virgin Mary an article of faith and the calling of the First Vatican Council, which established the doctrine of papal infallibility.

Prince Henry the Navigator (1394–1460): Inspired by his father's conquest of the Muslim city of Ceuta in North Africa in 1415, Henry initiated Portugal's exploration of the North African Coast. As general of a crusading order, he hoped to link with Prester John in Africa and with him drive the Moors from the southern coast of the Mediterranean and elsewhere. Henry contributed to the development of the art of navigation and cartography, establishing the school of navigators and mapmakers in his villa on the

Sagres Peninsula. From 1419 and until his death Henry invested and took part in several important expeditions of the African Coast. His sailors were among the first Europeans to discover the island of Madeira, the Azores, and several islands of the Cape Verde archipelago.

Ricardo, David (1772–1823): English economist, a founder of political economy, and at once a disciple and an opponent of Adam Smith. Ricardo's classic work, *The Principles of Political Economy*, appeared in 1817. His most important contributions were the theory of rent, the concept of comparative advantage, and, most importantly, the iron law of wages. The theory of rent holds that rent is conditioned by the advantages that one site has over another due to differing degrees of soil fertility: It is highest on the most fertile land, and declines on the worst quality land. Comparative advantage ensured that international trade would bring benefits for all countries. Ricardo believed that each country should specialize in making the products in which it possessed a comparative advantage; that is to say, what it could produce efficiently. He also, following Malthus, determined that if wages rose, they might reach the point at which nutrition of the poor would so increase their fertility that competition among them would decrease wages back to a subsistence level, with much dislocation and misery as a consequence. Industrial wages, then, should be constant at a point where the population of workers would also remain constant, that is, at a subsistence level. This iron law of wages was taken as truth by factory owners and many social theorists and politicians as evidence that there should be no intervention on behalf of the poor, as such good intentions would cause negative consequences for them.

Richelieu, Cardinal Armand-Jean de (1585–1642): French cleric and statesman who rose to power during the reign of Louis XIII, serving as a Secretary of State from 1616 until his death in 1642. Among Cardinal Richelieu's achievements were consolidation and centralization of the royal power; the destruction of political factions in France; French military alliances with several Protestant countries during the Thirty Years War; and the establishment in 1635 of the *Académie Française*, a learned society entrusted with the task of standardizing the French language. Richelieu was ruthless in his building of absolutism, paying little attention to the suffering of the poor or the rights of organizations outside the crown. He humbled the nobility and replaced them in the provinces with royal intendants and he weakened the powers of the French *parlements*. He was tolerant in religion, however, reissuing the edict of Nantes and showing generosity to the Huguenots.

Robespierre, Maximilien (1758–1794): Known among his contemporaries as the "Incorruptible," Robespierre was one of the key figures in the French Revolution and architect of the Terror. A disciple of Rousseau and leader of the Jacobins—a radical republican faction—he became a member of the legislative assembly in 1789, the year of the Revolution. In 1793, as France was threatened by the invading Austrian and Prussian armies, Robespierre was elected leader of the Committee of Public Safety, which was instrumental in establishing the Reign of Terror. In July 1794, after a period of violence incited by conflict among rival political factions and marked by mass executions of enemies of the revolution, Robespierre was deposed and guillotined, along with several other leaders of the Terror.

Rousseau, Jean-Jacques (1712–1778): Jean-Jacques Rousseau was one of the most influential thinkers and authors during the 18th-century Enlightenment. Born in Geneva, he fled that city for France, where he was supported by aristocratic female patrons. Having won the competition organized by the Academy of Dijon, he became a celebrated writer, music critic, composer, and journalist. Although a man of many talents, Rousseau was best known as a political theorist. He wrote *The Social Contract* (1762), an influential book in which Rousseau took the contract theory of Hobbes and Locke and altered it fundamentally by proposing that men and women in the state of nature were good and that society corrupted our natural virtue. Moreover, when the contract was made to form a society, sovereignty was not surrendered to a king, even one controlled by his subjects, but to the community itself which then became the sovereign General Will. This idea and his belief that virtue could be imposed if necessary and that French society was perhaps too far from nature and too corrupt to be reformed, except by an extraordinary Lawgiver, provided much support to the most radical leaders of the Revolution. Besides *The Social Contract*, Rousseau wrote in the same year *Emile* (1762), a treatise on education, and his *Confessions* (completed in 1769; first printed in 1782), one of Europe's great autobiographies.

Saint-Simon, Comte Henri de (1760–1825): Henri de Saint-Simon was an impoverished nobleman whose utopian, semi-mystical ideas of Christian-Scientific socialism were influential in the 19th century, forming the theoretical core of the eponymous movement of "Saint-Simonianism." His most influential work, *The New Christianity* (1825), proposed the reorganization of society with a ruling elite comprised of philosophers, engineers, and scientists and the creation of a new secular humanist religion with a priesthood of scientists to substitute for what he described as obsolete dogmas. Saint-Simon played a central role in the development of the social sciences, believing that society must be studied with the same rigor and methodology that scientists employed in investigating natural phenomena. Although Saint-Simon was one of the first to identify the conflict between capital and labor in industrializing Europe, his perspective remained essentially elitist.

Salutati, Coluccio (1331–1406): Trained as a notary, Salutati went on to hold various public offices, including the chancellorships of Todi (1367–1368), Lucca (1370), and Florence (1375–1406). A friend and correspondent of Petrarch, Salutati was a humanist scholar with an interest in classical literature, culture, and history who actively contributed to the revival, rediscovery, and translation of ancient texts. During his term as chancellor, humanism was institutionalized within the Florentine Republic, with Salutati hiring scholars trained in this tradition for positions in civic government. As a result, Florence became the leading center of humanism in Europe.

Smiles, Samuel (1812–1904): Scottish author and reformer, employed for some time as a journalist in Leeds before becoming secretary to a chain of railway companies. Beginning in 1859, Smiles authored a series of books on the topic of self-help, the characters of which were self-made working men who achieved all their goals in life and laid the foundations of Britain's industrial greatness. For the modern reader these works have come to exemplify traditional Victorian values of hard work, thrift, self-improvement, and earnestness. Although Smiles was criticized by socialists as an apologist for middle-class paternalism because of his emphasis on individual achievement, he was immensely popular and his *Self Help* was identified as a fundamental text of the second half of the 19th century.

Smith, Adam (1723–1790): Scottish philosopher and economist, considered the father of modern political economy. Smith's book *An Inquiry into the Nature and Causes of the Wealth of Nations* (1776) was an important landmark in the history of economics due to its convincing analysis of the mechanisms that drive the industrial economy, describing the economy in almost Newtonian terms of balance and natural forces such as supply and demand (the unseen hand). Smith was among the first thinkers to advocate a free market economy as more productive and more beneficial to society, opposing the prevalent theory of mercantilism and economic protectionism, which prescribed government regulation of the economy. He also formulated and advocated the importance of the division of labor in industry and manufacture to increase productivity.

Spencer, Herbert (1820–1903): English philosopher, sociologist, and one of the most energetic Victorian theorists of Social Darwinism. Spencer is known for having extended Darwin's natural selection into the realm of sociology and ethics, and for coining the famous phrase "survival of the fittest." He remained throughout his life an ardent opponent of imperialism and militarism, even though he grew conservative in his social and political views towards the end of his life. He was immensely popular both with contemporary intellectuals, the educated middle, and even working classes. Over a million of copies of his works were sold during his lifetime, and he was compared to Aristotle by some of his followers.

Stalin, Joseph (1878–1953): Joseph Stalin was the general secretary of the Central Committee, the chief executive body in the Soviet Union. He was also the leader of the Communist Party and to all intents and purposes the head of the Soviet Union between 1924 and 1953, having succeeded Lenin. Stalin eliminated Lenin's New Economic Policy, which allowed a certain degree of free trade and private property, replacing it with a "planned economy" (based on five-year plans), an economic system in which the central government decided on the production, distribution, and price of all goods and services. During the 1930s, Stalin launched the Great Purge, a campaign of repression to purge the Soviet Union of its "inner enemies" (so-called "enemies of the people"), resulting in hundreds of thousands of executions and in many more deaths in the Gulag. Despite a non-aggression pact, Hitler invaded Russia in 1941, bringing the Soviets into the war on the side of the allies. Russia suffered millions of casualties, but it was the Red Army that captured Berlin. To cement his power after the war, Stalin imposed communist rule over most of eastern Europe, forming the Soviet Bloc and initiating the Cold War.

Süleyman the Magnificent (1494–1566): The 10th sultan of the Ottoman Empire, ruling from 1520 until his death; he is considered the greatest sultan of his dynasty. Under his reign, most of the Middle East and parts of Eastern Europe were annexed to the Ottoman Empire, as well as territories in North Africa as far as Algeria, marking the greatest extent of Ottoman rule and his empire as the most powerful in the Western world. In 1521, Süleyman captured Belgrade and in 1523 succeeded in driving the Knights of Saint John of Jerusalem from Rhodes. In 1526 he annihilated the Christian army at Mohacs in Hungary, occupying the kingdom for some decades and besieging Vienna itself in 1529. He is known in the Muslim world as Suleiman the Lawgiver (*Kanuni*), on account of the wide-ranging legislative changes he instituted. He was a patron of culture, arts, and science, as well as a warrior.

Thiers, Adolphe (1797–1877): Prominent French politician and historian. During the July Monarchy (1830–1848), Thiers served as a prime minister to Louis-Philippe. In 1871, after the suppression of the Paris Commune of 1870, Thiers was elected provisional head of state, effectively the President of France; and it was he who had to make peace with the victorious Prussians and accept their humiliating terms after the Franco-Prussian War. He failed to secure the office of president when the Third Republic was established in 1873, yielding the office to his successor, Patrice MacMahon. Thiers was also a member of the *Académie Française*.

Turgot, Anne-Robert (1721–1781): French economist and royal minister, who became an early advocate of economic liberalism, advocating changes to the trade and fiscal policies of France in the 18th century. Turgot put forward these ideas in his entries in Diderot and d'Alembert's *Encyclopédie*. Turgot initially planned to enter the priesthood but in 1752 abandoned the seminary to enter the royal administration. As financial administrator of the impoverished province of Limoges in 1761–1773, he instituted reforms that resulted in dramatic improvements which brought him to the attention of the court. Louis XVI promoted Turgot to the position of comptroller-general, in which role he tried to reform royal taxation and to improve the conditions of both the rural peasantry and urban poor. However, his proposal to tax the privileged classes resulted in his being dismissed. His most important work is *Thoughts on the Creation of Wealth and its Distribution* (*Réflexions sur la formation et la distribution de richesses*) of 1766 which had considerable influence on Adam Smith.

Victor Emmanuel II of Italy (1820–1878): King of Sardinia, Piedmont, and Savoy, and, after the unification of Italy in 1861, the first king of Italy. He was greatly indebted to the diplomatic and military talents of his Prime Minister Camillo Cavour, who managed the policies of Italian unification for the House of Savoy and convincing the king to maintain liberal, secular policies to unite all Italian nationalists behind his cause. Victor Emmanuel supported Giuseppe Garibaldi's Expedition of the Thousand (1860–1861), which resulted in the fall of the kingdom of the Two Sicilies in southern Italy, a kingdom which Garibaldi then ceded to Victor Emmanuel. In 1870, when French troops were recalled to serve in the Franco-Prussian war, the king ordered his army to capture Rome and what remained of the Papal States, initiating a division between the Church and the liberal Italian monarchy that would endure until 1929. The capital and the royal court in 1871 moved from Florence to Rome. Victor Emmanuel became a symbol and a hero of the Risorgimento and contributed significantly to the creation of the modern Italian nation.

Victoria of England (1819–1901): Queen of the United Kingdom of Great Britain and Ireland and from 1876 the Empress of India. Reigning for more than 63 years, Victoria was the longest reigning monarch in Britain. Her sovereignty coincided with a time of great economic and cultural progress within the United Kingdom and the great expansion of the British Empire. Queen Victoria skillfully arranged marriages for her nine children and multiple grandchildren across the Continent, strengthening familial ties between royal dynasties and binding all Europe together. Her reign saw the establishment of Parliamentary democracy, with the extension of the franchise and a professional civil service. The Victorian period also witnessed the general and growing prosperity of the United Kingdom, which, because of improvements in medicine, social legislation, technology, and education, was shared more broadly than ever before.

Biographical Notes

Voltaire (1694–1778): Francois-Marie Arouet de Voltaire was a famous French man of letters and one of the leaders of the Enlightenment. He was born in a middle-class family—he added the aristocratic *particule* "de" to his own name—and educated by the Jesuits at the College Louis-le-Grand, intended by his father for a legal career. However, Voltaire chose literature as a career. He possessed a caustic wit and keen powers of observation and ridicule, which caused him both to be arrested and patronized by powerful men and women—the regent of France, the Duke d'Orleans, had him thrown into the Bastille, while later the mistress of Louis XV, Mme de Pompadour, secured for him a position at court. His natural spirit of skepticism and his recognition of the role played by the Church in the ancien régime made him increasingly hostile to religion. In place of revealed religion and ecclesiastical hierarchy, he proposed a natural religion, or deism, discussed particularly in his *Essay on the Customs and the Character of Nations* (*Essaie sur les moeurs*, 1756), and in *Candide, or Optimism* (1758). Voltaire spent much of his life outside of France for his own protection, corresponding widely, including with rulers such as Catherine the Great of Russia and Frederick the Great of Prussia, with whom he lived for a period before they quarreled. Perhaps Voltaire's greatest contribution was in the popularization of the central ideas of the Enlightenment through his witty books, entries in the *Encyclopédie,* and copious correspondence.

Wallenstein, Albrecht von (1583–1634): Talented Bohemian military commander who served the Holy Roman Emperor Ferdinand II during the early stage of the Thirty Years' War (1618–1648). Wallenstein was granted the title and authority of the Supreme Commander of the Imperial Armies, having raised a large and terrible private army, known for its ruthlessness and violence against both enemy soldiers and local inhabitants. In the campaign against the Swedish king Gustavus Adolphus, whom his soldiers killed at Lutzen in 1632, and later against the Protestant alliance, Wallenstein mystified his superiors by either not fully exploiting the possibilities to bring about a victory to the Emperor or by completely avoiding conflict. Worried that Wallenstein was secretly betraying the emperor, Ferdinand ordered the assassination of his able commander in 1634.

Wilson, Woodrow (1856–1924): Woodrow Wilson was the 28th president of the U.S. After serving as president of Princeton University from 1902–1910 and as governor of New Jersey from 1911–1913, he was elected president in 1913 and again in 1916. Wilson's second term was marked by U.S. involvement in the First World War, beginning in 1917. After the war, Wilson traveled to Paris to negotiate the Versailles treaties in 1919 and to agitate for the creation of the League of Nations, for which he was awarded the 1919 Nobel Peace Prize, despite the fact that the United States did not join. His refusal to recognize the secret treaties negotiated to bring previously neutral countries into the war against Germany greatly angered and destabilized Italy in particular, with unfortunate results. In 1919, after working hard to build popular support for the league in the U.S, Wilson suffered a stroke which left him partly paralyzed and required his wife to work in his place.

Zola, Émile (1840–1902): Zola was an eminent French writer and journalist of the latter half of the 19th century. His books, in the style of realism and naturalism, were powerful social commentaries, particularly *Nana*, about the corruption of elite Parisian society, and *Les Rougon-Macquart*, which chronicled the life of a bourgeois family under the Second Empire. Although Zola grew wealthy from his writings, he was vigorously hostile to the regime of Napoleon III and showed socialist sympathies, best reflected in his great 1885 novel, *Germinal*, describing a French miners' strike. Zola was also the courageous defender of Alfred Dreyfus, publishing in 1898 an open letter, "*J'accuse*," in which he declared that the accusation was a miscarriage of justice. The letter formed a turning point in the case and galvanized the anti-Dreyfusards. A republican and strongly anti-clerical, Zola's powerful pen made him many enemies, one of whom perhaps blocked up the chimney in his house, causing his death by carbon monoxide poisoning.

Zwingli, Ulrich (1484–1531): Preacher in Zurich and a leader of the Swiss Reformation. Strongly influenced by Erasmus and other Christian humanists, Zwingli attacked ecclesiastical abuses, advocated priestly marriage, and disputed Catholic dogma of the presence of Christ in the Eucharist. This brought him into conflict with other reformers, notably Luther. He also opposed the use of images in places of worship and introduced a new liturgy to replace the mass. In 1531, Zwingli was killed in the Battle of Kappel when the Catholic cantons of southern Switzerland attacked Zurich.

Bibliography

Adamson, John. *The Noble Revolt: The Overthrow of Charles I.* London: Orion, 2009. A fresh scholarly interpretation of the events surrounding Charles I's attempts at personal rule.

Andelman, David. *A Shattered Peace: Versailles 1919 and the Price We Pay Today.* New York: John Wiley & Sons, 2007. A clear discussion of how the failures of Versailles created the conditions not only for World War II but also for many of the present conflicts in Europe.

Arx, Paul von. *Progress and Pessimism: Religion, Politics, and History in Late Nineteenth Century Britain.* Cambridge MA: Harvard University Press, 1985. A complex book that integrates innate Victorian pessimism with the prevailing mood of optimism.

Ashton, Thomas. *The Industrial Revolution, 1760–1830.* New York and Oxford: Oxford University Press, 1998. The most recent edition of the best short discussion of the effects of industrialization.

Asprey, Robert. *The Reign of Napoleon Bonaparte.* New York: Basic Books, 2002. The sequel study of Napoleon as emperor of the French.

———. *The Rise of Napoleon Bonaparte.* New York: Basic Books, 2001. A detailed and insightful biography of Napoleon's early career.

Aydon, Cyril. *A Brief Guide to Charles Darwin, His Life and Times.* Philadelphia: Running Press Book Publishers, 2007. A popular but reliable study of Darwin in the context of his age.

Bainton, Roland. *Here I Stand: A Life of Martin Luther.* Peabody, Massachusetts: Hendrickson Classic Biographies, 2009. A new edition of the classic study of Luther and his revolution.

Bartlett, Robert. *The Making of Europe: Conquest, Colonization and Cultural Change, 950–1350*. Princeton: Princeton University Press, 1993. An interdisciplinary and challenging study of the making of Europe.

Barzun, Jacques. *Darwin, Marx, Wagner: Critique of a Heritage*. Reprint. Barzun Press, 2007. This reissue of the classic study of the influence of three of Europe's most revolutionary thinkers puts Darwin in the broader context of the intellectual and cultural history of his time.

Beales, Derek. *The Risorgimento and the Unification of Italy*. Harlow: Longman Publishing Group, 2003. A comprehensive but accessible study of the Risorgimento.

Begley, Louis. *Why the Dreyfus Affair Matters*. New Haven: Yale University Press, 2009. A brilliant analysis of the event, its causes and implications, written with conviction and clarity.

Bendersky, J.W. *A Concise History of Nazi Germany*. Lanham, MD: Rowman and Littlefield, 2006. A concise yet authoritative history of the rise and rule of the Nazis.

Bercé, Yves-Marie. *The Birth of Absolutism: A History of France, 1598–1661*. Tr. Richard Rex. New York: Palgrave-Macmillan, 1995. An engaging analysis of the development of royal absolutism and the policies of Richelieu and Mazarin.

Bergin, J. *Cardinal Richelieu: Power and the Pursuit of Wealth*. New Haven: Yale University Press, 2009. A new and scholarly study of the career of Richelieu in the context of his times.

Biagini, E.F. *Liberty, Retrenchment and Reform: Popular Liberalism in the Age of Gladstone, 1860–1880*. Cambridge: Cambridge University Press, 2004. A thorough study of why Liberalism in late Victorian Britain became a popular movement and persuasive political ideology.

Bibliography

Blom, Philipp. *Enlightening the World: Encyclopédie, The Book That Changed the Course of History.* New York: Palgrave-Macmillan, 2005. A richly textured account of the making and the makers of the Encyclopedia.

Boer, Pim den, et al. *The History of the Idea of Europe.* New York: Routledge, 1995. This collection of essays puts the idea of Europe in context from the church fathers, through the Enlightenment and 19th century into the present.

Bosworth, R.J.B. *Mussolini's Italy: Life Under the Fascist Dictatorship, 1915–1945.* New York: Penguin Press, 2007. A wide-ranging study of Italian life under fascism written by one of the pre-eminent scholars of modern Italy.

Bouwsma, William. *John Calvin: A Sixteenth-Century Portrait.* Oxford: Oxford University Press, 1989. Bouwsma places Calvin in the context of European thought and culture.

Braddick, Michael. *God's Fury, England's Fire: A New History of the English Civil Wars.* London: Penguin Books, 2009. The English civil wars of the 17th century seen through the perspective of those who experienced them.

Brucker, Gene. *Renaissance Florence.* Berkeley-Los Angeles-London: University of California Press, 1983. Still the best brief history of Florence during the period of the Renaissance.

Burke, Peter. *Culture and Society in Renaissance Italy.* 2nd edition. Princeton, Princeton University Press, 1999. An invaluable discussion of Italian Renaissance culture in its historical context.

Chartier, Roger. *The Cultural Origins of the French Revolution.* Bicentennial Reflections on the French Revolution. Durham NC: Duke University Press, 1991. A broadly based discussion of the many cultural and intellectual circumstances that made the French Revolution possible, if not inevitable.

Creighton, Mandell. *A History of the Papacy from the Great Schism to the Sack of Rome.* 3 vols. Montana: Kessinger, 2007–**200**9. A new edition of an old but still magisterial and detailed study of the Church in crisis.

The Darwin Reader. Edited by Mark Ridley. New York: Norton, 1996. A splendid collection of Darwin's essential works with interpretive essays.

Davis, Lance and Robert Huttenback. *Mammon and the Pursuit of Empire: The Political Economy of British Imperialism, 1860–1912.* Cambridge; Cambridge University Press, 2009. An economic study of the race for empire.

De Grand, A. *Italian Fascism: Its Origins and Development.* Lincoln NA: University of Nebraska Press, 2000. A brief analysis of the rise of fascism as a nationalist movement opposed to socialism.

Dear, Peter. *Revolutionizing the Sciences: European Knowledge and Its Ambitions, 1500–1700.* Princeton: Princeton University Press, 2009. A revisionist study of how the scientific revolution had deep roots in European philosophy and knowledge of nature.

Doyle, William. *The Oxford History of the French Revolution.* Oxford: Oxford University Press, 2003. The authoritative study of the events of the revolution.

Duby, G. *Rural Economy and Country Life in the Medieval West.* Trans. by C. Postan. Pennsylvania, University of Pennsylvania Press, 1998. A new edition of the standard study of the medieval agricultural economy.

Duffy, Eamon. *The Stripping of the Altars: Traditional Religion in England, 1400–1580.* New Haven, CT: Yale University Press, 2005. A detailed and brilliant discussion of the Church in England—both Catholic and reformed—and the role it played in people's lives.

Engels, Friedrich. *The Condition of the Working Class in England.* Oxford World's Classics. Edited by D. McLellan. New York and Oxford: Oxford University Press, 2009. A new edition of the work by Marx's collaborator on the conditions of the poor in mid-19th-century Britain.

Evans, R. *The Third Reich in Power.* New York: The Penguin Group, 2006. A study of the administration and government of Germany under the Nazi dictatorship, illustrating the party's complete control over every aspect of German life.

Eyck, Erich. *Bismarck and the German Empire*. New York: Norton, 1964. The most accessible but authoritative study of Bismarck and his times.

Farmer, Alan and Andrina Stiles. *The Unification of Germany 1815–1919*. 3rd revised edition. UK: Hodder Education, 2007. A short, accessible but useful study of the process and events of the unification of Germany.

The Freud Reader. Edited by Peter Gay. New York: Norton, 1995. A comprehensive collection of Freud's most important writing on many subjects with an excellent introduction and commentary.

Fritze, Ronald. *New Worlds: The Great Voyages of Discovery 1400–1600*. Westport, CT.: Praeger, 2003. This book puts the voyages of discovery into the context of European medieval and early modern culture and values, as well as describing the voyages themselves.

Gay, Peter. *Schnitzler's Century: The Making of Middle-Class Culture 1815–1914*. New York: W.W. Norton, 2002. A revisionist study of bourgeois culture in Europe in the 19th century by a distinguished scholar.

Guarnieri, C.J. *The Utopian Alternative: Fourierism in Nineteenth-Century America*. Ithaca: Cornell University Press, 1994. Still the best study on the widespread influence of utopian socialism in the United States during the 19th century.

Hadley, Elaine. *Living Liberalism: Practical Citizenship in Mid-Victorian Britain*. Chicago: University of Chicago Press, 2010. The most recent study on Victorian Liberalism.

Haigh, Christopher. *English Reformations: Religion, Politics, and Society under the Tudors*. Oxford: Oxford University Press, 1993. A revisionist and insightful study of religion, politics and society in Tudor England.

Hawkins, M. *Social Darwinism in European and American Thought,*

1860–1945: Nature as Model and Nature as Threat. Cambridge: Cambridge University Press, 1997. A broad and comprehensive discussion of the influence of Social Darwinism.

Henry, John. *The Scientific Revolution and the Origins of Modern Science*. New York: Palgrave-Macmillan, 2008. An excellent short history of the beginning of the modern science.

Hollingdale, R.J. *Nietzsche: The Man and his Philosophy*. Cambridge: Cambridge University Press, 2001. The best introduction to Nietzsche and his work, from a sympathetic perspective.

Holt, Mack. *The French Wars of Religion, 1562–1629*. New Approaches to European History. Cambridge: Cambridge University Press, 2005. This engaging narrative of a complex time places the wars of religion in France in a wider historical context.

The Idea of Europe: From Antiquity to the European Union. Edited by Anthony Pagden. Cambridge: Cambridge University Press, 2002. The best contemporary collection of essays by leading scholars to discuss the question of European identity from antiquity to the present.

Jones, P. *The Italian City-State from Commune to Signoria*. Oxford: Oxford University Press, 1997. A broadly based study of the development of Italian cities and towns in the Middle Ages and early Renaissance.

Kaeuper, Richard. *Chivalry and Violence in Medieval Europe*. Oxford: Oxford University Press, 1999. This text convincingly makes the connection between violence and feudal power.

Kahan, Alan. *Liberalism in Nineteenth-Century Europe: The Political Culture of Limited Suffrage*. New York: Palgrave-Macmillan, 2003. An important study of Liberal attitudes across Europe centred on the question of suffrage.

Kenez, Peter. *A History of the Soviet Union from the Beginning to the End.* Cambridge: Cambridge University Press, 2006. An impressive synthesis of Russian history from the revolution until the fall of communism.

Kershaw, Ian. *Hitler: A Biography.* New York: Norton, 2008. An abridged. highly readable edition of the magisterial two-volume study of Hitler and the Nazi regime.

Kissinger, Henry. *The World Restored: Metternich, Castlereagh, and the Problems of Peace, 1812–22.* London: Weidenfeld and Nicholson, 2000. A scholarly study of the diplomacy at Vienna and beyond by an architect of U.S. foreign policy and co-winner of the 1973 Nobel Peace Prize.

Kitchen, Martin. *Europe Between the Wars.* 2nd ed. Harlow: Longman Publishing Group, 2006. A very accessible study of the political, economic, social and cultural conditions in Europe between the wars.

Kolb, Eberhard. *The Weimar Republic.* 2nd ed. New York: Routledge, 2004. An English translation of the latest version of this authoritative study of Weimar experiment.

Korner, Axel. *The Politics of Culture in Liberal Italy: From Unification to Fascism.* New York: Routledge, 2008. The role of reinterpreted culture binding together the new Italian nation after unification.

Ledger, Sally and Roger Luckhurst, eds. *The Fin de Siècle: A Reader in Cultural History, c. 1880–1900.* Oxford: Oxford University Press, 2000. A wide-ranging interdisciplinary approach to the period.

Lee, Stephen. *European Dictatorships 1918–1945.* New York: Routledge, 2008. A wide-ranging study of the rise of dictators—whether royal, fascist or communist—in the years after the Great War.

———. *Gladstone and Disraeli.* New York: Routledge, 2005. A comparison of the two dominant political figures of in Britain in the last third of the 19th century.

Lefebvre, Georges. *The Coming of the French Revolution*. Princeton: Princeton University Press, 2005. The best available discussion of the situation in France before and at the outbreak of the Revolution.

Leonard, Mark. *Why Europe Will Run the 21st Century*. New York: PublicAffairs™, 2006. A brief but extremely provocative book written by a leading policy analyst that argues that Europe is positioned to assume a new role in world economic, political, and diplomatic affairs.

Loeb, Lori. *Consuming Angels: Advertising and Victorian Women*. New York and Oxford: Oxford University Press, 1994. A wonderfully illustrated study of the rise of advertising directed at women and the creation of the middle-class definition of gentility.

Lopez, Robert. *The Commercial Revolution of the Middle Ages, 950–1350*. Cambridge: Cambridge University Press, 2008. A synthetic analysis of the complexity of the medieval European economy by one of the best economic historians.

MacCulloch, Diarmaid N.J.. *The Reformation: A History*. New York: Penguin Group, 2003. The best overview of the events of the European Reformation in context by the best living historian of the period.

Gordon, Bruce. *The Swiss Reformation*. Manchester: Manchester University Press, 2002. A wide-ranging and detailed discussion of the Reformation in Switzerland.

MacLeod, Christine. *Heroes of Invention: Technology, Liberalism and British Identity, 1750–1914*. Cambridge: Cambridge University Press, 2008. A study of the interaction between technology, progress, liberalism, and national self perception in Britain.

MacMillan, Margaret. *Paris 1919: Six Months That Changed the World*. New York: Random House, 2003. The best and most insightful analysis into the negotiations at Versailles.

Marx, Karl, and Friedrich Engels,; *The Communist Manifesto*. Edited by David McLellan. Oxford World's Classics. New York and Oxford: Oxford University Press, 1998. The short text that brought Marx to the leadership of the international socialist movement in 1848.

Matthew, Colin. *The Nineteenth Century: The British Isles 1815–1901*. Short Oxford History of the British Isles. New York and Oxford: Oxford University Press, 2000. A comprehensive survey of Britain in the 19th century, with significant social, economic, and cultural material.

McCormick, John. *Understanding the European Union: A Concise Introduction*. New York: Palgrave-Macmillan, 2008. An excellent introduction to the development and policies of European integration.

McLellan, David. *Young Hegelians and Karl Marx*. Aldershot: Ashgate, 1993. A short discussion of Marx's ideas in the context of the intellectual world of 19th-century Europe.

Meyer, G.J. *A World Undone: The Story of the Great War, 1914 to 1918*. New York: Delacorte Press, 2007. A seamlessly integrated, detailed study of the events of the Great War, not just limited to Europe.

Mill, John Stuart. *The Basic Writings of John Stuart Mill: On Liberty, The Subjection of Women and Utilitarianism*. New York: Modern Library Classics, 2002. The basic texts of Liberal thought by its most articulate 19th-century spokesman.

Mollat, Guillaume. *The Popes at Avignon, 1305–1378*. New York: Harper & Row, 1965. Mollat's text has not been surpassed.

Moore, Robert. *The First European revolution, 970–1215*. Oxford: Oxford University Press, 2000. The best analysis of the rise of feudal society.

More, Charles. *Understanding the Industrial Revolution*. London: Routledge, 2000. A synthetic approach to industrialization, placing the events in a broad context.

Nauert, Charles. *Humanism and the Culture of the Renaissance*. Cambridge: Cambridge University Press, 1995. An elegant, short but comprehensive study of the subject.

O'Malley, John. *Trent and All That: Renaming Catholicism in the Early Modern Era*. Cambridge, MA: Harvard University Press, 2002. An insightful, wide-ranging discussion of how the Catholic Church responded to the challenges of the age of the Reformation and the nation state.

Outram, Dorinda. *The Enlightenment*. Cambridge: Cambridge University Press, 2005. A short but comprehensive introduction to the ideas and context of the Enlightenment.

Pagden, Anthony. *Lords of all the World: Ideologies of Empire in Spain, Britain and France c.1500–c.1800*. New Haven: Yale University Press, 1998. This book describes the different ways and arguments these countries used to legitimate their seizure and subjugation of lands and peoples

Pangle, Thomas L. *Montesquieu's Philosophy of Liberalism: A Commentary on the Spirit of the Laws*. Chicago: Chicago University Press, 1989. Still the best study of Montesquieu's integration of natural rights, liberalism and history.

Parker, Geoffrey. *The Thirty Years' War*. London and New York: Routledge, 1997. The classic, elegant political study of the war.

Phillips, Margaret Mann. *Erasmus and the Northern Renaissance*. Totowa, N.J.: Rowman and Littlefield, 1981. The best short introduction to the culture of Christian humanism.

Pickering, Mary. *Auguste Comte: An Intellectual Biography*. 2 vols. Cambridge: Cambridge University Press; vol. 1—1993; vol. 2—2009. Now the definitive study in English of Comte and positivism.

Pipes, Richard. *A Concise History of the Russian Revolution*. Vintage Books. New York: Knopf Doubleday Publishing Group, 1996. An abridged version of Pipes' magisterial two-volume history of the revolution: readable and authoritative.

Rapport, Michael. *1848: Year of Revolution*. New York: Basic Books, 2009. A breezy, readable narrative of the year of revolution.

———. *Nineteenth Century Europe*. Palgrave History of Europe. New York: Palgrave-Macmillan, 2005. A survey of the continent, including social, political, economic and cultural information.

Reston, James. *Defenders of the Faith: Charles V, Suleyman the Magnificent, and the Battle for Europe, 1520–1536.* London: Penguin, 2009. The book focuses on the campaigns of Suleyman the Magnificent to conquer Vienna and central Europe.

Ritter, Alan. *Jean-Jacques Rousseau's Political Writings.* Norton Critical Editions. New York: Norton, 1987. An excellent selection of Rousseau's political writings with reactions from Voltaire to Tolstoy.

Ryder, A.J. *The German Revolution of 1918: A Study of German Socialism in War and Revolt*. Cambridge: Cambridge University Press, 2008. A study of the revolutions in Germany in 1918 in the context of the history of Marxist political agitation and politics before the war.

Sargent, W.L. *Robert Owen and His Social Philosophy*. Ann Arbor: University of Michigan Press, 2009. A new study of Owen and his ideas on social justice.

Schama, Simon. *Citizens: A Chronicle of the French Revolution.* London: Vintage Publications, 1990. An engrossing and readable popular history of the revolution written by a leading historian.

Schorske, Carl. *Fin-De-Siècle Vienna: Politics and Culture*. Vintage Books. New York: Alfred A. Knopf Inc., 1980. Still the best narrative of the culture and society of late Habsburg Vienna.

Scurr, Ruth. *Fatal Purity: Robespierre and the French Revolution*. New York: Henry Holt and Company Inc., 2006. A fascinating portrait of the revolution as seen through the life of Robespierre, architect of the Terror.

Smith, Crosbie. *Engineering Empires: A Cultural History of Technology in Nineteenth-Century*. New York: Palgrave-Macmillan, 2005. A well integrated study of the relationship between advances in technology and the search for empire.

Sperber, Jonathan. *The European Revolutions, 1848–1851*. Cambridge: Cambridge University Press, 2006. A comprehensive but accessible discussion of the revolutions that consumed Europe.

Spufford, P. *Power and Profit: The Merchant in Medieval Europe*. London: Thames and Hudson, 2003. A recent and valuable discussion of the commercial revolution of the later Middle Ages.

Thompson, E.P. *The Making of the English Working Class*. New York: Peter Smith Publisher, 1999. The reissue of Thompson's influential study from a leftist perspective of the conditions of the poor in Britain.

Tuchman, Barbara. *A Distant Mirror: The Calamitous Fourteenth Century*. A Ballantine Book. New York: Random House, 1987. A popular, if depressing, survey of the century of change, plague and war.

———. *The Guns of August*. Novato, CA: Presidio Press, 2004. A popular and compelling but reliable history of the war in a new reprint volume.

Voltaire, François-Marie Arouet *Candide and Other Stories*. Oxford: Oxford University Press, 2008. A selection of Voltaire's most important and engaging texts.

Weitz, Eric. *Weimar Germany: Promise and Tragedy*. Princeton: Princeton University Press, 2009. An excellent and insightful study of the culture of the Weimar republic and the reasons for its failure.

Bibliography

Wheatcroft, Andrew. *The Enemy at the Gate: Habsburgs, Ottomans, and the Battle for Europe*. New York: Basic Books, 2009. A new and informative study of the Turkish threat to Europe in the early modern period.

Wilson, Peter. *The Thirty Years War: Europe's Tragedy*. Cambridge, MS: Harvard University Press, 2009. A fresh study of this cataclysmic event from the perspective of political, social and economic, as well as religious, history.

Zamoyski, Adam. *Rites of Peace: The Fall of Napoleon and the Congress of Vienna*. New York: Harper & Row Publishers, 2008. A popular historian offers a brisk narrative of the events and personalities of 1814–1815.

Notes

Notes

Notes